ANATOMY AND PHYSIOLOGY
APPLIED TO OBSTETRICS

EX LIBRIS

D1331819

Anatomy and Physiology Applied to Obstetrics

SYLVIA VERRALLS SRN SCM MTD

Formerly Principal Midwifery Tutor
North Middlesex Hospital

SECOND EDITION

CHURCHILL LIVINGSTONE
EDINBURGH LONDON MELBOURNE AND NEW YORK 1987

CHURCHILL LIVINGSTONE
Medical Division of Longman Group UK limited

Distributed in the United States of America by
Churchill Livingstone Inc., 1560 Broadway, New York,
N.Y. 10036, and by associated companies, branches
and representatives throughout the world.

First published 1969 (Pitman Publishing Ltd)
    Reprinted 1973
    Reprinted 1974
    Reprinted 1975
    Revised reprint 1977
Second reprint 1980
    Reprinted 1981
    Reprinted 1982
    Reprinted 1983
    Reprinted 1984
    Reprinted 1987 (Churchill Livingstone)
    Reprinted 1988

ISBN 0-443-03879-1

British Library Cataloguing in Publication Data

Verralls, Sylvia
    Anatomy and physiology applied to obstetrics. – 2nd ed.
    1. Generative organs, Female
    2. Women – Physiology
    I. Title
    612.6'2   QP259

Printed in Great Britain at The Bath Press, Avon

Contents

Internal Organs.

Preface

This short work is intended as a guide to the practical application of anatomy in order that the knowledge gained by the midwifery student will be related to the clinical situations that she (or he) meets every day. The book pre-supposes, as is usual in our midwifery schools, that those who read it will be gaining practical experience in clinics and on the wards before the theoretical syllabus laid down by the Central Midwives Board has been covered. It is therefore designed to be used as a handbook to supplement clinical experience.

Wherever possible the simple tabulated method used to describe each organ is the same. This list of headings has been found very helpful by students in assisting them with recollection of facts when revising.

Simple blackboard diagrams have, in the main, replaced the more detailed illustrations usually found in anatomy textbooks. These are diagrams that even the least artistic of students should be able to reproduce and understand.

This revised edition comes at the request of those tutors and students who have asked for amendments and additions. Thanks to the publishers and their medical artist, as many requests as possible have been included, without the size and price of the book being too greatly increased. We trust that this new edition will prove just as popular as the first.

My thanks are due to the production staff of Pitman Medical, and to all those tutors and students who have offered constructive criticism. The tutors and students at St John's Hospital, Chelmsford, and Southlands Hospital, Shoreham, have been particularly helpful.

I would also like to thank the Central Midwives Board for the continued use of questions from some of their examination papers.

1

The Female Breasts

The female breasts, also known as the mammary glands, are the accessory organs of reproduction.

Situation

One breast is situated on each side of the sternum, and extends from the level of the second to the sixth rib. The breasts lie in the superficial fascia of the chest wall, over the pectoralis major muscle, and are stabilised by suspensory ligaments.

Shape

Each breast is a hemispherical swelling, and has a tail of tissue extending towards the axilla.

Size

The size varies with each individual, and with the stage of development as well as with age.

Gross Structure
(Figure 1.1)

The axillary tail is the tail of tissue extending towards the axilla.

The areola is a circular area of loose pigmented skin, about 2.5 cm (1 in) in diameter at the centre of each breast. It is a pale pink colour in a fair skinned woman, darker in a brunette; the colour deepening with pregnancy. Within the area of the areola lie approximately twenty sebaceous glands.

The nipple lies in the centre of the areola at the level of the fourth rib. A protuberance about 6 mm (0.25 in) in length, com-

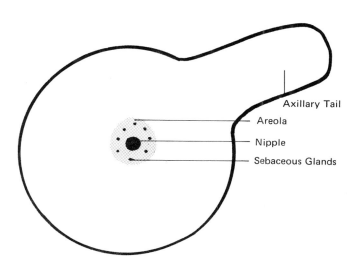

Figure 1.1
Gross Structure of the
Breast

posed of pigmented erectile tissue, it is a highly sensitive structure. The surface of the nipple is perforated by small orifices, the opening of the lactiferous ducts.

Microscopic Structure
(Figure 1.2)

The breast is composed largely of glandular tissue, but also of some fatty tissue, and is covered with skin. This glandular tissue is divided into lobes which are completely separated by bands of fibrous tissue. The internal structure is said to resemble the segments of a halved grapefruit or orange. Each lobe is a self-contained working unit and is composed of the following:

1. *Alveoli*: the milk secreting cells, sometimes called *Acini*.
2. *Lactiferous tubules*: small ducts which connect the alveoli.
3. *Lactiferous duct*: a central duct into which the tubules run.
4. *Ampulla*: the widened-out portion of the duct where milk is stored.
5. *Continuation of lactiferous duct*: extending from the ampulla and opening on to the nipple.

Figure 1.2
Microscopic Structure of
the Breast

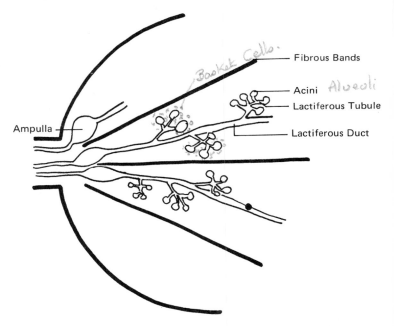

Blood Supply

Blood is supplied to the breasts by the **internal mammary artery**, the **external mammary artery**, and the **upper intercostal arteries**.

Venous drainage is through corresponding vessels into the **internal mammary** and **axillary veins**.

Lymphatic Drainage	Into the **axillary glands,** and into the **portal fissure of the liver.** The lymphatic vessels of each breast communicate with one another.
Nerve Supply	The function of the breasts is largely controlled by hormone activity, but the skin is supplied by branches of the thoracic nerves and there is some sympathetic nerve supply especially around the areola and nipple.
Function	To supply milk for the infant.

STAGES OF BREAST DEVELOPMENT

At Birth	The breast tissue is confined to the nipple area and only the nipple is prominent. Sometimes during the first few days of life, the breast tissue is enlarged and fluid is secreted because of the action of circulating maternal hormones in the infant's blood stream. This condition requires no treatment, for the swelling will subside as maternal hormones are withdrawn and the infant's own hormone level becomes adjusted.
At Puberty	When the hormone level begins to alter at puberty and usually before the onset of menstruation, the breast tissue begins to bud. Slow development continues as the gland tissue, the lactiferous tubules, and ducts continue to proliferate and the amounts of fatty and fibrous tissue are increased. At the same time, the nipple and areola become more pronounced.
Childbearing Years	In the latter half of the menstrual cycle many women, during their childbearing years, complain of breast changes similar to those taking place in pregnancy. These changes are caused by the progesterone produced by the corpus luteum, and soon disappear with the onset of the menstrual flow and decreasing progesterone levels.
In Pregnancy	Pregnancy changes occur first in response to oestrogen, then to progesterone from the corpus luteum, and then to hormones from the developing placenta. Stimulus by oestrogens results in development of the nipple and areola, and growth of the lactiferous tubules and ducts. Progesterone causes proliferation of the alveoli in preparation for milk production. Visible pregnancy changes are noted more readily in a primigravida.
Sixth to Eighth Weeks of Pregnancy	The soft tissues of the breast become more nodular to the touch. There is a sensation of fullness, tenderness, and of tingling—many women dislike their breasts being touched at this period of pregnancy. As the blood supply is increased, the subcutaneous veins become more clearly visible.

Twelfth Week

Pigmentation of the nipple and areola deepens to a permanent brown discoloration, and both become more accentuated. The sebaceous glands lying within the areola enlarge and secrete an oily substance which lubricates the nipple in preparation for breast feeding. At this stage, these glands are known as Montgomery's tubercles.

After Twelve Weeks

Colostrum, a clear watery fluid, is secreted by the breasts and can be expressed from the nipple. Its main function is to clear the lactiferous ducts and tubules of dead epithelial tissue and make way for a free flow of milk.

After Sixteen Weeks

A mottled area surrounding the areola appears and is known as the secondary areola. It is more obvious in dark-haired women. Following childbirth it disappears.

Following Delivery

Approximately three days following delivery of the infant, the breasts secrete the milk. It is at this stage only that the breasts can be said to have reached their full development.

Colostrum
Composition

Protein (8%)	Colostrum corpuscles
Fat	Leucocytes
Lactose	Dead epithelial casts
Mineral salts	

Function

The function of the colostrum is to keep the lactiferous tubules and ducts clear, and to act as an aperient for the infant, emptying the bowel of meconium.

Although fluid volume is small, the high protein content allows for adequate nutrition. Newborn infants may require extra fluid intake in the form of boiled water in the first forty-eight hours of life, but the greater majority do not require complementary feeds of cow's milk.

PHYSIOLOGY OF LACTATION

Hormone Control

When separation and expulsion of the placenta has taken place, an alteration in the oestrogen-progesterone balance occurs, resulting in the release of the hormone prolactin from the anterior pituitary gland. Oestrogen suppresses the action of prolactin, and so it is not until about three days following delivery that the mother's milk 'comes in'.

Theoretically, if suppression of lactation is desired, then oestrogens can be administered in the form of drugs such as hexoestrol or stilboestrol to inhibit the action of prolactin and so prevent a flow of milk. However, because of the risk of deep venous thrombosis and possible breast cancer this treatment is not now used.

Production of Milk

As the increased blood supply is circulated through the breast, essential substances for milk formation are extracted. Fatty globules and protein molecules form within the base of the secretory cells, distend the alveoli, and push their way through to the lactiferous tubules. Lactation therefore depends not only upon the fine adjustment of the essential hormones, but also upon a good blood supply circulating through the breast.

Passage of Milk

Two factors are involved in the transit of milk from the secretory cells to the nipple:

1. Back Pressure

The force of new globules forming in the cells pushes the foremost ones into the lactiferous tubules and then to the lactiferous duct.

2. Neuro-Hormonal Reflex

When the baby is put to the breast, the rhythmical sucking movement empties the ampulla and large lactiferous ducts, causing them to contract and more milk is thus forced down towards the nipple. As the nipple is stimulated by the suckling there is a nervous reflex action, the direct result of which is the liberation of an oxytocic secretion from the posterior lobe of the pituitary gland. This, in turn, causes further contraction of the lactiferous vessels and still more milk flows to the nipple. This same oxytocic secretion also causes the uterine muscles to contract, and so aids involution of that organ during the puerperium.

Maintenance of Milk

Supply is maintained in response to demand. The more often the baby is put to the breast, the better is the milk supply. If the baby is not put to the breast, the milk supply will fail.

Two factors are essential for maintenance, stimulus and complete emptying of the breast:

1. Stimulus

The stimulus of the infant's gums on the breast. The main force of suction being on the skin of the areola results in the neurohormonal reflex. If the infant cannot go to the breast, then stimulation is applied by emptying the breast by hand.

2. Complete Emptying of Breast

Following each feed, the breast must be completely emptied. If the infant does not remove all the milk available, then the mother should be taught to express it by hand. Regular expression of residual milk ensures a free flow as well as providing a new supply.

Composition of Milk

Protein	1.5%	Water	87.8%
Fat	3.5%	Salts	0.2%
Lactose	7.0%		

Breast milk is an alkaline fluid, bluish white in colour, with a specific gravity of 1031. It contains 140 joules per 50 cm^3 (20 calories per fluid ounce).

THE PROMOTION OF BREAST FEEDING

Preparation for successful breast feeding should begin soon after the twelfth week of pregnancy, although many expectant mothers in these early weeks are as yet undecided, or tend to shy away from the subject. Some of the following advantages might profitably be discussed at a private interview, and the mother encouraged to talk about her own hopes or fears.

No mother must be forced or frightened into breast feeding when this is really against her own wishes, but many can be encouraged not only to try, but to persevere and enjoy the experience, with the assistance and guidance of a wise midwife.

Advantages
Correct Constituents

Human milk provides food constituents in the correct balance for human growth. Cow's milk, on the other hand, must be modified in many ways before it can be tolerated by a human infant, whose rate of growth is much slower than that of the calf. Babies fed on cow's milk tend to gain weight much more quickly than those who are breast fed, but such weight gain does not necessarily indicate healthy progress.

Another factor which has received a great deal of publicity is that some babies have an intolerance to the protein in cow's milk. The inhalation of this milk following regurgitation is said to have been the cause of many infant cot deaths. This topic is one which might well be discussed at parentcraft classes but should never be used in a way which will frighten nervous mothers into breast feeding against their inclination.

Less Risk of
Contamination

Milk taken directly from the breast by the infant is less likely to be contaminated by pathogenic organisms, and the incidence of neonatal infections is therefore reduced. In particular, the risks of gastro-enteritis are very much reduced among breast fed infants: this method of feeding has proved to be the surest way of reducing deaths from this disease.

Breast milk is also known to contain important antibodies and conveys immunity from some diseases during the first few weeks of life.

In an age when the dangers of contamination from radioactive fall-out are much discussed, it should be brought to notice that breast milk contains far less Strontium 90 than does cow's milk. Therefore, the newborn can be given some degree of protection by breast feeding.

Convenience

It has been said that time and money can both be saved by breast feeding. Feeds do not require preparation and there are no utensils to be cleaned and sterilised, but in a modern household these are not always very important factors. Neither is breast feeding any kinder to the household budget, because although there are no infant milk preparations to be purchased, the mother herself should be drinking extra milk and eating extra protein.

Physical Factors

The neuro-hormonal reflex resulting in the 'let down' of milk has already been described. The oxytocin released during this reflex action also stimulates uterine contractions and so aids involution of the uterus.

Quite recently it has been shown by statistics that the incidence of carcinoma of the breast is increased among those mothers who have lactation suppressed instead of allowing it to become fully established, but it would be better not to discuss this fact with an expectant mother.

Emotional Factors

To be breast fed is a baby's birthright—it gives him a feeling of security and a good foundation for the development of all personal relationships. To his mother it should bring that sense of final achievement which is the culmination of childbearing.

When the expectant mother has expressed a desire to attempt breast feeding then it is most likely that she will succeed. Undoubtedly, difficulties do sometimes arise and the mother who begins in a spirit of unwilling sacrifice is much more likely to fail. Other important factors which affect the failure or success of breast feeding are the standards of antenatal preparation and the post-natal supervision of the mother until she feels wholly confident that she is able to satisfy the demands of the hungry infant. Ante-natal patients might be given an opportunity to visit a post-natal ward to discuss, and perhaps watch, successful breast feeding with newly delivered mothers whom they have met at classes.

Antenatal Care
Nutrition

It is not necessary to make any great change in dietary habits if the expectant mother is already a well-nourished woman, but the antenatal clinic provides an excellent opportunity for revising the dietary habits of those women who do not eat very sensibly. An increase in the daily intake of protein is advised for all expectant mothers, and an extra pint of milk in addition to the usual intake is suggested unless a special diet has been ordered. This extra milk also provides additional calcium, a mineral which is stored in preparation for lactation. Iron is also stored to supply the infant's needs while he is being breast fed and, therefore, the mother's diet should also contain daily some foods which contain this substance. Iron tablets should be taken throughout the antenatal period to supplement the dietary intake.

Examination of the Breasts—Size

By the fourteenth week of pregnancy, the bust measurement is likely to have increased by about 5 cm (2 in), and at term the overall increase averages 10 cm (4 in). Lack of development indicates immaturity and is not favourable for milk secretion. An increase of more than 10 cm reveals a degree of hypertrophy which might necessitate the suppression of lactation.

—Skin Texture and Tone

The skin of the breast should be examined for its elasticity and tone. Thin skin which can be picked up loosely between the thumb and forefinger is skin which will stretch easily when the breast is filled with milk. Thick, inelastic skin is more likely to cause difficulty, as tension arises in the breast causing oedema of the lactiferous cells and ducts. This is known as engorgement.

—Skin Pigmentation

A dark haired woman has a much deeper degree of skin pigmentation on the nipple and areola. This offers a good deal of protection to the nipples when the baby starts feeding, and the woman rarely complains of sore nipples. A fair haired woman lacks this protective pigmentation, and therefore needs to carry out greater nipple care.

—Nipples

The superficial appearance of the nipple is not always a good guide and it should be tested for its degree of protraction. The thumb and forefinger are used to imitate the action of the baby's jaws. If the nipple remains flat on the skin surface or if it is withdrawn below the level of the skin (inverted or retracted), treatment is necessary. Even if only one nipple is malformed, both nipples should be treated similarly. Glass or plastic shells (as recommended by the late Dr Waller of Woolwich) are given to the patient and she is advised to wear these over the nipple, inside her brassiere. At first they are worn for a few minutes daily, the time being gradually increased until they are worn for the greater part of the day. The shells create suction and therefore pull the nipple out.

The nipples should also be examined for dried secretions of colostrum and epithelial cells. Such secretions cause clogging of the ducts which open on to the nipple and can also cause soreness. The mother is shown how to cleanse the nipple, using cotton wool soaked in olive oil, and is advised how to prevent a recurrence.

Hygiene and Daily Care

The breasts and nipples should be washed carefully each day, using soap and hot water, then carefully dried with a soft towel. Simple breast massage and expression of colostrum is taught and carried out from the twenty-eighth week of pregnancy onwards. This treatment keeps the lactiferous ducts and orifices clear in preparation for the milk flow, and is a sure method of helping to prevent engorgement of the breasts during the first few days of the puerperium. If the mother is fair skinned she should also be taught to prepare her nipples for the suckling of her infant. Each nipple should be gently rolled between the well-lubricated thumb and forefinger for just a few seconds each day.

Breast care should not be elaborate or time-consuming, for then it is likely to be neglected altogether.

Support

Because of their increasing size and weight the breasts must be supported throughout pregnancy with a well-fitting uplift brassiere. Lack of such support causes the breasts to hang down, and the lactiferous tubules and ducts kink, resulting in stasis of secretions and blockage of ducts. It is possible to obtain a brassiere which will expand up to 10 cm (4 in), and can therefore be worn throughout pregnancy. As it has a front fastening, this is also very suitable for use in the lactation period. For comfort, the brassiere should have wider shoulder straps and a deep diaphragm band.

Post-natal Care
General Health

The mother who is in good health, having had a normal labour and delivery, and who has been adequately prepared mentally and physically for breast feeding during the antenatal period, begins the lactational phase with every advantage. Her general health should be maintained, and anaemia prevented at this time by the same well-balanced diet that she was eating prior to delivery. Nourishing fluids should be taken as part of the extra milk allowance and iron tablets should be continued. Adequate rest and avoidance of worry are extremely important factors, and the atmosphere surrounding the mother should be kept as tranquil as possible.

Support

Following delivery, an uplift brassiere should be worn continuously, a breast binder being supplied to those mothers who have no suitable supporting garments. This is especially important on the second and third days when the breasts begin to fill, the reasons for good support having been already mentioned.

Hygiene and Daily Care

The brassiere or breast binder must be clean and changed daily, or as necessary. The mother's hands and breasts must be washed before feeding, and the midwife must always wash her hands before touching the mother's breasts. Between the second and seventh days the breasts should be emptied by hand in order to stimulate lactation. An inspection of breasts and nipples should be made twice daily in order to assess the amount of milk and to exclude abnormalities of the breast and sore nipples. Between these inspections the mother should be asked to report painful breasts or sore nipples. Following feeds, a prophylactic cream can be applied to the nipples—more especially if the mother is fair-skinned and liable to skin abrasion—and the nipples should then be covered with sterile breast pads before the brassiere or breast binder is re-applied.

Feeding Technique

Following normal labour and delivery the baby should be put to the breast in the labour ward. If labour has not been normal then it should be done as soon as the condition of mother and baby allows. There can be no definite ruling about this, but in these early hours the mother normally longs to cuddle her baby to her breast and to feed him. There is little fluid in the breast so soon after delivery, but the infant's instinctive sucking reflex should be satisfied too. The first few feeds should be enjoyed by mother and baby. They should be fully supervised by a skilled midwife who can 'fix' the baby correctly. By the third or fourth day when the mother's milk has come in, the baby will have been trained to feed smoothly and steadily. Feeding times should be graduated so that the nipple slowly becomes accustomed to friction and so becomes toughened. Sucking for too long or sucking an empty breast will both cause soreness of the nipples. 'Demand feeding' can be instituted in these early days; the mother being advised at first not to feed her infant more than three-hourly, and to wake him if he sleeps for more than five hours. The baby will soon settle into his own approximate four-hourly routine.

When feeding the baby, the mother should be in a comfortable position and the baby well supported with a clear airway. The areola as well as the nipple should be taken into his mouth, so that the gums apply pressure to the ampullae where milk is stored. At the end of the feed at each breast the baby should be sat up straight with his back well supported and encouraged to bring up any 'wind' he might have swallowed with his feed. An average guide is given below:

First Day   Four-hourly practice feeds allowing 3 minutes at each breast. If the baby is thirsty, extra water can be given by spoon.

Second Day   5 minutes allowed at each breast.

Third Day   7 minutes allowed at each breast.

Fourth Day   10 minutes allowed at each breast if breasts are full, otherwise delay 10 minute period until the fifth day.

To sum up, then, successful breast feeding is dependent upon four main factors:

1. The mother's wholehearted desire to feed the baby herself.
2. The anatomical structure of the breasts and nipples.
3. The standard of antenatal preparation.
4. The supervision of feeding in the early days by a skilled midwife who can offer supervision without domination.

SPECIMEN
QUESTIONS
Describe the anatomy of the female breast. What changes take place in the breasts during pregnancy?

Describe the female breast. What steps can be taken to assist successful breast feeding?

Describe the anatomy of the breast. Tabulate the indications and contra-indications for breast feeding.

What can be done during pregnancy and after delivery to help the establishment of breast feeding?

Describe the changes which take place in the breast during pregnancy. What anatomical defects of the breast make breast feeding difficult? How would you deal with these?

Describe the anatomy of the female breast. Discuss the management of excessive fullness of the breasts in the early days of lactation.

Describe the anatomy of the breasts. What changes take place during pregnancy? What advice can be given to the expectant mother in preparation for successful breast feeding?

2

The Normal Female Pelvis

Situation

The pelvis articulates with the fifth lumbar vertebra above, and with the head of each femur in the right and left acetabulum. The weight of the trunk is therefore transmitted through the pelvis to the legs.

Shape

It is similar to that of a bony basin and gives protection to the pelvic organs.

Size

The pelvic girdle is the largest formation of bone in the body.

Gross Structure
The Sacrum

This consists of five fused sacral vertebrae, four pairs of holes being formed where the vertebrae join with each other. Blood vessels, nerves, and lymphatics pass through these holes.

The hollow of the sacrum is the anterior surface of this roughly triangular shaped bone: it is smooth and concave. **The alae of the sacrum** are the widened out pieces of bone on each side of the first sacral vertebra giving it the appearance of wings. **The promontory of the sacrum** is the centre point of the upper border of the first sacral vertebra, and protrudes over the hollow of the sacrum.

The sacral canal runs through the centre of the bone and opens at the level of the fifth sacral vertebra. It makes a passage for the spinal cord which carries the spinal nerves. At the level of the second and third sacral vertebrae the nerves spread out to form the **cauda equina**. During labour, some obstetricians introduce local anaesthetic into the **caudal canal**. The nerves below the second sacral vertebra are thus temporarily paralysed and, although the patient remains fully conscious and co-operative, the pain of uterine contractions is relieved.

The Coccyx

Four fused coccygeal vertebrae make this tiny bone triangular in shape with the base lying uppermost and articulating with the sacrum. Muscles are attached to its tip.

Right and Left Innominate Bones (Figure 2.1)

Before the age of twenty-five these bones are not completely ossified. Each is made up of three separate parts which meet in the cup-shaped depression known as the **acetabulum**. These three parts are named the **ilium, ischium,** and **pubis**.

—the Ilium

This is the bone of the flank and is the upper, flat portion. It forms the upper two-fifths of the acetabulum. On the inside it is

Figure 2.1
The Innominate Bone

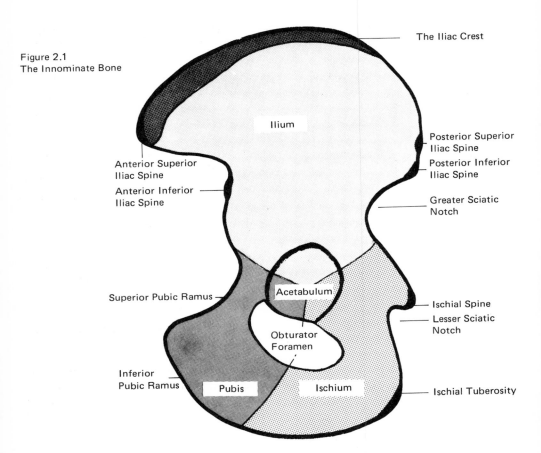

The Iliac Crest

Ilium

Posterior Superior
Iliac Spine

Posterior Inferior
Iliac Spine

Anterior Superior
Iliac Spine

Anterior Inferior
Iliac Spine

Greater Sciatic
Notch

Superior Pubic Ramus

Acetabulum

Ischial Spine

Lesser Sciatic
Notch

Obturator
Foramen

Inferior
Pubic Ramus

Pubis   Ischium

Ischial Tuberosity

smooth and concave, but the outside is rough and makes an attachment for the muscles of the buttocks.

The upper border of bone, the **iliac crest**, can be felt quite easily if the hands are placed on the hips. Where the iliac crest ends at the front is known as the **anterior superior iliac spine**. About 2.5 cm (1 in) below the superior spine is a small projection called the **anterior inferior iliac spine**. The **posterior superior iliac spine** is where the iliac crest ends at the back. Two small dimples on the right and left just above the cleft of the buttocks mark the area of these spines on a living person. The **posterior inferior iliac spine** marks the upper border of the **greater sciatic notch**, through which the sciatic nerve passes.

—the Ischium (Bone of the Seat)

This is the lowest part of the innominate bone and forms the lower two-fifths of the acetabulum. The **ischial tuberosity** is the body of the ischium, and it is upon the ischial tuberosities that we sit. About 2.5 cm (1 in) above the ischial tuberosity the **ischial spine,** which divides the greater and lesser sciatic notches, can be found.

—the Pubis

This is the smallest of the three components of the innominate bone, and forms the remaining lowest fifth of the acetabulum. The right and left pubic bones unite with each other anteriorly in the square-shaped **pubic body.** They are fused by a pad of carti-lage called the **symphysis pubis.** Extending upwards from the pubic body, the **superior ramus** unites with the ilium to form the **iliopectineal eminence.** The **inferior ramus** extends downwards to unite with the ischium. The right and left inferior (or descending) rami form the **pubic arch.** The space surrounded by the inferior and superior pubic rami is known as the **obturator foramen.**

The Four Pelvic Joints
The Two Sacroiliac Joints

These lie between the bodies of the first two sacral vertebrae and the upper surface of the ilium. They are slightly movable joints and are surrounded and supported by ligaments.

The Symphysis Pubis

This is the pad of cartilage lying between the bodies of the pubic bones. It is almost 4 cm (1.5 in) in length, and has supporting ligaments around it.

These three joints all increase their power of movement during pregnancy, because the hormone progesterone causes relaxation and softening of all smooth muscle.

The Sacrococcygeal Joint

Situated between the lower border of the sacrum and the upper border of the coccyx, the sacrococcygeal joint is surrounded by ligaments and is capable of allowing the coccyx to tilt backwards. This movement is greatly increased during labour, thus allowing more room for the fetal head as it passes through the birth canal.

The Pelvic Ligaments

These are the ligaments which support and surround the pelvic joints, the sacro-iliac ligaments being the strongest in the body.

The **sacro-tuberous ligament** stretches from the lower border of the sacrum to the ischial tuberosity. Running beneath the sacro-tuberous ligament is the **sacro-spinous ligament,** which ex-tends from the lower border of the sacrum to the ischial spine. **Poupart's ligament,** also known as the **inguinal ligament,** extends between the anterior superior iliac spine and the body of the pubis. Except for a small opening which allows the passage of blood vessels, nerves, and lymphatic vessels, the **obturator mem-brane** fills the obturator foramen.

Models of the pelvis should be handled daily by the student so that she becomes thoroughly familiar with each of the anatomical landmarks that have been mentioned.

Divisions of the Pelvis   The **brim** of the pelvis divides it into two parts, the false and the true pelvis. The **false pelvis** lies above the pelvic brim and is of little importance in midwifery. The **true pelvis** includes the pelvic brim and all the bone that lies below it. It is described as having a **brim, cavity,** and an **outlet,** and forms the curved canal through which the fetus must pass to be born.

The Brim or Inlet   This is almost round in shape in the normal female pelvis, and
(Figure 2.2)   eight points can be demonstrated on it:

1. Promontory of the sacrum.
2. Ala of the sacrum.
3. Sacro-iliac joint.
4. Iliopectineal line.
5. Iliopectineal eminence.
6. Inner border of the superior pubic ramus.
7. Body of the pubic bone.
8. Upper border of the symphysis pubis.

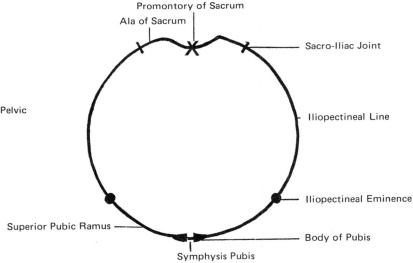

Figure 2.2
Landmarks of the Pelvic
Brim

The Cavity   The cavity extends from the brim of the pelvis above, to the pelvic outlet below. Formed by the hollow of the sacrum, the **posterior wall** is approximately 11 cm (4.5 in) in length. The **anterior wall** is formed by the symphysis pubis and is approximately

3.8 cm (1.5 in) long. The **lateral walls** are formed by an imaginary line drawn across:

1. The greater sciatic notch.
2. The back of the acetabulum.
3. The obturator foramen.
4. The back of the body of the pubic bone.

The Anatomical Outlet
(Figure 2.3)

This is bounded by:

1. The lower border of the symphysis pubis.
2. The inferior pubic rami.
3. The ischial tuberosities.
4. The sacro-tuberous ligament.
5. The tip of the coccyx.

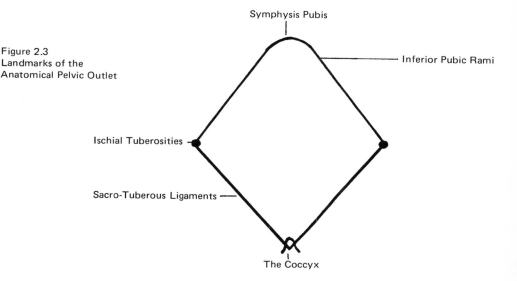

Figure 2.3
Landmarks of the
Anatomical Pelvic Outlet

Symphysis Pubis

Inferior Pubic Rami

Ischial Tuberosities

Sacro-Tuberous Ligaments

The Coccyx

These are all fixed points and useful landmarks for taking pelvic measurements and, because the coccyx can tip backwards and the ligaments are capable of stretching, there is more room for the fetus to pass than is at first apparent. The available room is therefore known as the **obstetrical outlet**.

The Obstetrical Outlet

Its landmarks are:

1. The lower border of the symphysis pubis.
2. The ischial spines.
3. The sacro-spinous ligament.
4. The lower border of the sacrum.

Measurements of the Pelvis
The Brim
(Figure 2.4a)

The distance between the promontory of the sacrum and the inner upper border of the symphysis pubis is known as the **antero-posterior diameter** (or **true conjugate**) and it should not be less than 11 cm (4 in). The **oblique diameter** is the distance between the sacro-iliac joint and the opposite iliopectineal eminence: it should not be less than 12 cm (4½ in).

Measured between the two widest points of the pelvic brim, the **transverse diameter** should measure at least 13 cm (5 in). (In the true female pelvis this is right across the centre of the pelvis). The measurement taken between the promontory of the sacrum and either iliopectineal eminence, and which should be at least 9.5 cm (3¾ in), is known as the **sacrocotyloid diameter**.

The Cavity
(Figure 2.4b)

The **antero-posterior diameter** is taken from the junction of the second and third sacral vertebrae to the mid point of the symphysis pubis. The **oblique** is measured at the same level in the pelvis as the antero-posterior diameter, and runs parallel to the oblique diameter of the pelvic brim: there are no fixed points to measure between.

In theory, the **transverse** diameter is a measurement taken between the two points farthest apart on the lateral pelvic walls. As there are no fixed points in the cavity these measurements cannot be accurately assessed but, as the cavity is circular, all diameters must be equal and they should all be at least 12 cm (4½ in).

The Outlet
(Figure 2.4c)

Measured from the lower border of the symphysis pubis to the lower border of the sacrum, the **antero-posterior** diameter should measure not less than 13 cm (5 in). The **oblique** is impossible to measure accurately because the sacro-tuberous ligaments stretch as they are distended by the fetal head. Nevertheless, it is accepted as lying parallel to the oblique diameters of the brim and cavity, and should be at least 12 cm (4½ in) long. The **transverse** diameter is estimated between either the ischial tuberosities or the ischial spines (both measurements being the same in the normal pelvis); this diameter should be 11 cm (4 in) at the minimum.

Two other measurements must be mentioned, the diagonal conjugate and the obstetrical conjugate. The **diagonal conjugate** can be assessed by vaginal examination and indicates the size of the pelvic brim. It is the distance between the lower border of the symphysis pubis and the promontory of the sacrum. The **obstetrical conjugate** is a measurement made between the inner surface at the centre of the symphysis pubis and the promontory of the sacrum.

All these measurements can be made accurately only by X-ray pelvimetry. The minimal measurements of the normal European female pelvis have been recorded here, but measurements vary considerably among the different races and even among women of the same race. This must be remembered in the cosmopolitan populations of today. In recent years, it seems also that the size of the female pelvis has increased in all countries of the world.

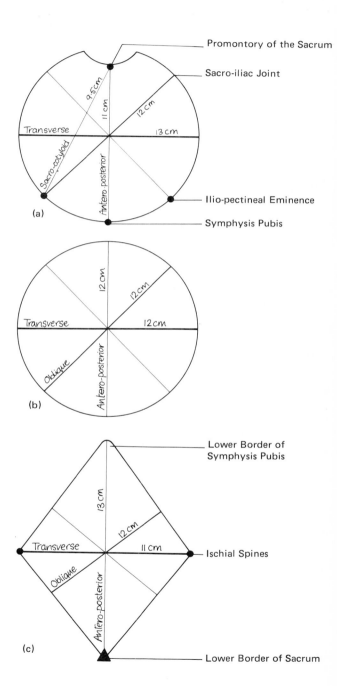

Figure 2.4
Measurements of the
Pelvis: (a) the brim,
(b) the cavity, (c) the
outlet

Table 2.1 Table of Measurements

	AP	Oblique	Transverse
Brim	11 cm (4 in)	12 cm (4½ in)	13 cm (5 in)
Cavity	12 cm (4½ in)	12 cm (4½ in)	12 cm (4½ in)
Outlet	13 cm (5 in)	12 cm (4½ in)	11 cm (4 in)

Note. These measurements are accepted as being the normal minimum.

Planes of the Pelvis
(Figure 2.5)

The planes of the pelvis are imaginary flat surfaces drawn at the level of the brim, cavity, and outlet. It has been shown here that the planes are of differing size, therefore they must each also be of differing shape.

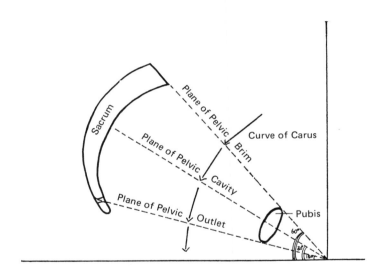

Figure 2.5
Planes of the Pelvis

When a person is standing upright, the plane of the pelvic brim makes an angle of 60° with the floor. Because the pelvis is a curved canal, the angles of the brim, cavity, and outlet must be different too, i.e.

The angle of the plane of the pelvic brim with the floor   = 60°
The angle of the plane of the cavity with the floor   = 30°
The angle of the plane of the outlet with the floor   = 15°

The **curve of Carus** is a line drawn at right angles to each of these planes, and is said to be the path which the fetus takes as it travels through the birth canal.

CLINICAL ASSESSMENT OF THE PELVIS

General Examination

At the patient's first visit to the antenatal clinic the following observations must be made:

1. Height ⎫
2. Weight ⎬ both recorded on the notes.
3. Waist measurement.
4. Shoe size.

These observations give a general impression of the patient's proportions, e.g. a very tall woman with tiny feet is not well proportioned, neither is a very short, stout woman, especially if she also has broad shoulders and thick hips.

The pupil midwife must practise this observation and always be alert for the patient who walks with a limp or who has muscle wasting of the legs. These may give an indication of congenital hip deformity, anterior poliomyelitis, and other conditions which will cause consequent pelvic deformities. This type of observation is especially important if, because of language difficulties, it is impossible to take a full medical history. Whenever it is possible the patient should be asked if she has ever been involved in an accident or received injuries to her spine, pelvis or legs.

Obstetric History

A careful history should be taken of previous labours and deliveries. If the patient has previously had a normal labour and delivery following a forty-week gestation period, and if the infant weighed at least 3 kg, it may be accepted that her pelvis is of adequate size. Should she be a primigravida, not have delivered a fair sized infant, or perhaps have a previous history of instrumental delivery or Caesarean section, then it cannot be assumed that her pelvis will be adequate and further observations and investigations become of vital importance.

External Measurements

These are rarely used in countries where more accurate means of pelvic assessment are available, but are often used by midwives working alone in remote areas overseas. The measurements are by no means accurate but will give an approximate size and shape of the pelvis and reveal any gross disproportion. Three measurements are taken using an instrument called a pelvimeter.

Interspinous Diameter

The points of the pelvimeter are placed one over each anterior superior iliac spine and the distance between them is normally about 25.5 cm (10 in).

Intercristal Diameter

The points of the pelvimeter are moved upwards over the iliac crests and the measurement between the two widest points, usually about 28 cm (11 in), is recorded. There is normally a difference of 2.5 cm (1 in) between these two diameters. If the difference is greater than 2.5 cm then a 'flat' pelvis which is contracted at the brim should be suspected.

External Conjugate

The patient is turned to lie on her side. One point of the pelvimeter is placed over the centre of the upper border of the symphysis pubis and the other point is placed over the tip of the spine of the fifth lumbar vertebra. (This is found by marking a point between the two dimples made by the posterior superior iliac spines and then moving upwards for about 2.5 cm. This measurement is usually about 19 cm (7½ in). To allow for subcutaneous tissues, 9 cm (3½ in) is subtracted and the resultant figure gives an approximate estimation of the antero-posterior diameter of the brim.

No pelvimeter is necessary for the fourth assessment, the **transverse of the outlet**. The patient lies in position as for vaginal examination. The midwife, wearing a glove, makes her hand into a fist and places it between the patient's ischial tuberosities. It should be possible for this diameter to admit the four knuckles of the clenched fist. Each midwife should know the measurement of her own knuckle, usually 7.5–9 cm (3–3½ in). Allowing for subcutaneous tissues, the actual measurement is therefore approximately 10–11.5 cm (4–4½ in) between these bony tuberosities.

Abdominal Palpation

A pelvis cannot be said to be adequate until the widest transverse diameter of the fetal head has passed through the pelvic brim. Once the head has passed through these bony borders, it should be able to pass through the cavity and the outlet, where some of the borders, being ligaments, are capable of distension. The only exception occurs when there is a contracted outlet, recognisable by sharp prominent ischial spines or by a narrow pubic arch.

It is therefore important that at the thirty-sixth to thirty-seventh week of pregnancy, the abdomen is palpated to see if the fetal head is 'engaged' or can be made to 'engage', i.e. the widest transverse diameter can be pushed through the pelvic brim. All patients should be seen by an obstetrician for this examination so that adequacy of the pelvis can be confirmed.

Vaginal Examination

Unless there is a previous history of abortion, the doctor usually performs a vaginal examination on every new patient attending the antenatal clinic. This is not only to confirm the pregnancy but also to exclude abnormalities of the pelvis and its contents. A further examination is made at the thirty-sixth to thirty-seventh week of pregnancy to ensure that the fetal head will pass through the pelvis and to assess the pelvic brim, cavity, and outlet.

Assessment of the Brim
(Figure 2.6a)

If the head is not already through the pelvic brim an assessment is made by estimating the **diagonal conjugate**. The two index fingers are placed in the vagina, running them immediately beneath the symphysis pubis and attempting to reach the promontory of the sacrum. The thumb is placed externally over the symphysis pubis. If the sacral promontory cannot be felt, then the diagonal conjugate, and therefore the brim of the pelvis, is said to be adequate. If the sacral promontory can be felt, then the diagonal

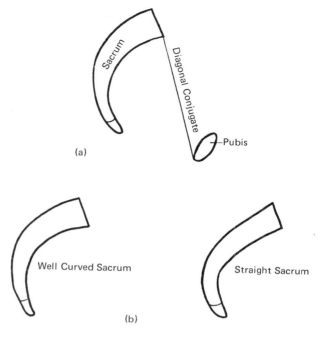

(a)

Figure 2.6
Assessment of the Pelvis
by Vaginal Examination:
(a) the brim (b) the cavity
(c) the outlet

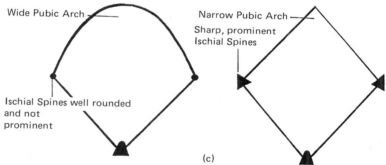

conjugate is reduced in diameter, and the doctor making this examination will refer the patient to a consultant obstetrician for further investigations.

Assessment of the
Cavity
(Figure 2.6b)

If the fetal head is not in the pelvis it is possible to feel the curve of the sacrum. It should be well hollowed and not straight. The doctor then seeks for the **sacro-spinous ligament** and this should be the width of two fingers across the greater sciatic notch.

Assessment of
the Outlet
(Figure 2.6c)

The fingers are run to the lateral borders of the outlet, feeling for the **ischial spines** which should be well rounded and not sharp or projecting inwards.

The **pubic arch** should be well rounded so that two fingers can be placed in the angle of the arch. If this is not possible, then a narrow sub-pubic angle is diagnosed, thus limiting the room available at the outlet. Before completing this examination, the transverse diameter of the outlet (mentioned previously) should be assessed.

X-Ray Pelvimetry

This is the most accurate method of estimating the relationship between the maternal pelvis and fetal head.

Before the examination is carried out, the patient's bladder and rectum should both be emptied. A standing lateral picture is taken so that the radiologist can measure the antero-posterior diameters of the pelvic brim, cavity, and outlet. These measurements are then compared with the size of the fetal skull. In consultation with the radiologist the obstetrician is then able to decide whether a vaginal delivery should be attempted, or whether elective Caesarean section must be carried out.

VARIETIES OF PELVIS

It is possible to tell the sex, and sometimes the race, of a person by the shape of the pelvis. The normal classification used is that of Caldwell and Molloy.

There are four main groups, namely:

1. Gynaecoid.
2. Android.
3. Platypelloid.
4. Anthropoid.

Other types of pelvis described are, Robert, Naegele, and Justo-minor.

Gynaecoid Pelvis
(Figure 2.7)

This is another name for the normal female pelvis which has been described. To sum up briefly:

The brim is round.
The cavity has a well curved sacrum.
The outlet has ischial spines which are well rounded and neither sharp nor prominent. The pubic arch has a well rounded angle.

Because the pelvis is well rounded anteriorly, the fetus presents with the most rounded part of his head (the occiput) anteriorly, this being the most favourable position at the start of labour.

Android Pelvis
(Figure 2.8)

In the male type of pelvis, the bones are heavier than those of the female pelvis and there are several distinctive characteristics.

The brim is heart-shaped, making the fore pelvis very narrow. The transverse diameter (taken between the two widest points on

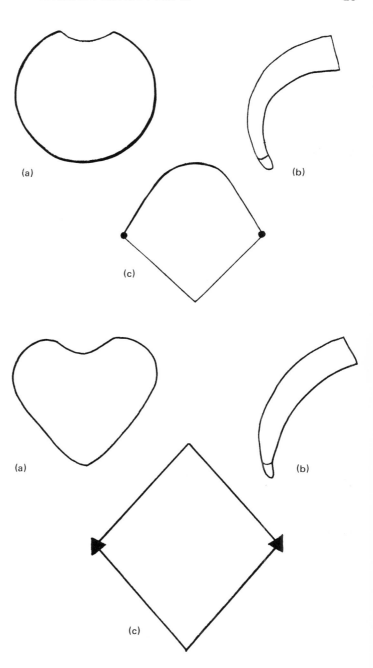

Figure 2.7
The Gynaecoid Pelvis:
(a) the brim, (b) the
cavity, (c) the outlet

Figure 2.8
The Android Pelvis: (a)
the brim, (b) the cavity,
(c) the outlet

the brim) does not cross the centre of the pelvis but is much nearer the sacrum, thus proving that there is more space available at the back of the pelvis than at the front.

In the cavity the hollow of the sacrum has a very poor curve, indeed it is almost straight. The sacrum is also larger, giving the cavity a deep funnel-shaped appearance. The greater sciatic notch is also narrower than that of the gynaecoid pelvis.

In the outlet, because the fore pelvis is narrow, the inferior pubic rami meet together at a much sharper angle making a sharper sub-pubic angle, and thus reducing the available space. The ischial spines are sharp and turn inwards, and so the transverse diameter of the outlet is reduced.

Effect on Labour

The fetus presents with the occiput lying posteriorly where there is more room. However, even if the head negotiates the brim and cavity, it may become obstructed at the outlet where the prominent ischial spines reduce the transverse diameter, and then instrumental delivery becomes necessary.

Platypelloid Pelvis
(Figure 2.9)

This may be due to rickets when the following characteristics can be described:

The brim has a short antero-posterior diameter, but the transverse diameter is lengthened giving the brim a kidney- or bean-shaped appearance.

In the cavity at this level, the diameters are affected in the same way as those at the brim, but there is usually room for the fetal head.

The outlet. Because the pelvis is shallow, the inferior rami meet at a very gradual angle to form a very wide pubic arch, and therefore a capacious outlet.

The simple flat pelvis should also be described here. At the brim it resembles the rachitic pelvis, having a reduced antero-posterior diameter. Unlike the rachitic pelvis, however, the diameters of the cavity and outlet are smaller than normal.

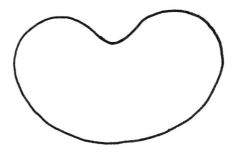

Figure 2.9
Brim of the Platypelloid
Pelvis

Effect on Labour

The fetal head finds difficulty in engaging in the pelvis and usually presents with the long diameter of the head across the transverse diameter of the brim where most room is available. Three things may happen as labour advances:

1. With uterine contractions the fetal head is pushed to and fro between the sacral promontory and the symphysis pubis. It thus

'rocks and rolls' through the brim to the cavity. The skull bones overlap each other with this pressure, and the process is known as **asynclitism.**

2. The fetal head may be obstructed in the narrow diameter of the brim, and uterine contractions cause it to extend as it descends (normally, flexion occurs as the head descends). This results in a **face presentation.**

3. If the brim is greatly contracted, the fetal head remains floating high above it and **Caesarean section** becomes imperative. This is a fairly common occurrence in countries where there is very little antenatal care, but it is a condition which should be recognised by the last weeks of pregnancy here in Great Britain. Caesarean section is then carried out before the patient goes into labour, exposing mother and infant to a lesser risk of traumatic injury.

Anthropoid Pelvis
(Figure 2.10)

Very tall, long legged women appear to have this type of pelvis. It is quite common in the women of South Africa.

The brim is oval in shape having a long antero-posterior diameter but a reduced transverse.

The cavity is adequate in all diameters but it is rather deep.

The outlet is adequate in all diameters with the pubic arch being rather wide.

Figure 2.10
Brim of the Anthropoid
Pelvis

Effect on Labour

The fetus presents with the long diameter of the head in the antero-posterior diameter where it can be most easily accommodated. The occiput more often lies in the hollow of the sacrum than directly anterior. The fetus then passes through the pelvis, remaining in the same position and so delivers **face to pubes** instead of **face to perineum.**

Robert Pelvis

This pelvis has no wings (alae) of the sacrum and is therefore contracted in all diameters. It is a type very rarely seen and is the result of congenital abnormality. Caesarean section is always necessary for delivery.

Naegele Pelvis

There is only one wing of the sacrum in this pelvis, giving it an obliquity. The cause may be due to congenital abnormality but could have been caused by injury. A true Naegele pelvis is rarely seen, but some obliquity of the pelvis can also occur in a woman who has walked with a limp for many years. Delivery by Caesarean section is always indicated.

Justo-minor Pelvis

This is a miniature gynaecoid pelvis. It is truly gynaecoid in shape but all diameters are equally reduced. It is to be found in the petite woman who is less than 1.5 metres tall. The type of labour and delivery will depend upon the size of her husband and, therefore, the size of the baby. She may deliver a small baby vaginally with very little trouble. On the other hand, a larger baby may require a forceps delivery or even Caesarean section.

Contracted Pelvis

This is one in which one or more of the essential diameters (i.e. antero-posterior, oblique, or transverse of brim, cavity or outlet) is reduced by 1 cm or more.

These then are the main categories of pelvis, but it must be remembered that the majority of abnormalities cannot be clearly defined as belonging to one of these groups. Most abnormal pelves have just one of these varying attributes.

The **straight sacrum** associated with the android pelvis is probably one of the most common variations that complicates obstetrics.

Describe the bony pelvis. In your examination of the patient what might make you suspect the presence of a pelvic abnormality?

Describe the anatomy of the skeletal pelvis. What methods are adopted during pregnancy to ascertain that the pelvis is adequate for the passage of the child?

Describe the true pelvis. How may a narrow sub-pubic arch complicate labour?

Write short notes on:

1. The pelvic brim.
2. Outlet of the bony pelvis.
3. The true conjugate.

Describe the classification of pelves according to Caldwell and Molloy.

Describe the brim, cavity, and outlet of the female pelvis. How may the pelvis be clinically assessed during the antenatal period?

Describe the bony pelvis. What is the obstetrical significance of the pelvic landmarks?

3

The Pelvic Floor

The outlet of the bony pelvis is filled with soft tissues which support the pelvic and abdominal organs. These tissues do not form a flat floor but a gutter-shaped structure which is higher anteriorly than posteriorly. Three canals, each with an external orifice, run through the tissues: the urethra, the vagina, and the rectum. There are six layers of tissue (Figure 3.1):

1. An outer covering of skin.
2. Subcutaneous fat.
3. Superficial muscles enclosed in fascia.
4. Deep muscles enclosed in fascia.
5. Pelvic fascia thickened to form pelvic ligaments.
6. Peritoneum.

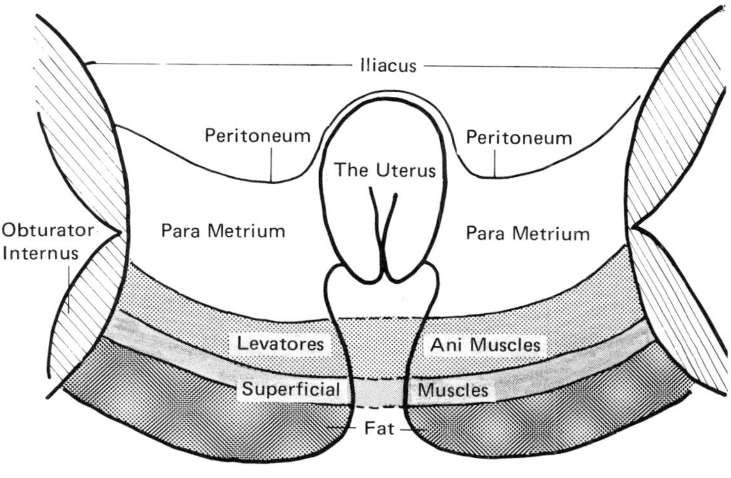

Figure 3.1
Tissue Layers of Pelvic
Floor

Superficial Pelvic Floor Muscles
(Figure 3.2)
Transverse Perinei

One muscle arises from each ischial tuberosity and they meet in the centre of the perineal body.

Bulbo-cavernosus

Two muscles arise in the centre of the perineum, they pass one on each side of the urethra and vagina encircling the orifices and then insert into the pubic bones.

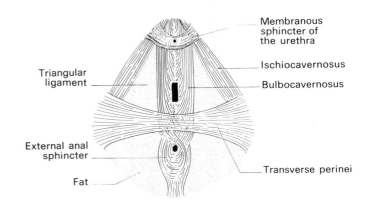

Membranous
sphincter of
the urethra

Ischiocavernosus

Triangular
ligament

Bulbocavernosus

External anal
sphincter

Transverse perinei

Fat

Figure 3.2
Superficial Muscles of the
Pelvic Floor

Ischio-cavernosus

One muscle runs from each ischial tuberosity to the pubic bones.
This still leaves four areas at the outlet not filled with tissue: the
posterior areas are filled with **fat**; the anterior areas are filled by
the **triangular ligaments**.

*The Membranous
Sphincter of the
Urethra*

This is formed by two bands of muscle that pass in front and
behind the urethral orifice.

The Rectal Sphincter

This is a ring of muscle encircling the anus.

**Deep Pelvic Floor
Muscles**
(Figure 3.3)

These are three pairs of muscles which all have their insertion
around the coccyx and, because of this, they are sometimes called
the **coccygeus muscles**. Their anatomical name is the **levatores ani
muscles**, and they are about 5 mm thick.

Figure 3.3
Deep Muscles of the Pelvic
Floor (Levatores Ani
Muscles)

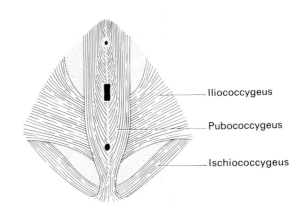

Iliococcygeus

Pubococcygeus

Ischiococcygeus

Ilio-coccygeus

This arises from a point on the **ilium** known as the **white line of fascia,** and it passes backwards to the **coccyx.**

Ischio-coccygeus

This arises from each **ischial spine,** and passes to the **coccyx** and lower border of the **sacrum.**

Pubo-coccygeus

Each muscle arises from the **pubic bone** and passes backwards surrounding the urethra, vagina, and rectum before inserting into the coccyx. In Perineum

THE PERINEAL BODY

Situation

It lies between the vaginal and rectal canals.

Shape

Is triangular, the base being the skin and the apex pointing upwards.

Size

Each side of the triangle is approximately 3.8 cm (1.5 in) in length.

Structure
(Figure 3.4)

There are three layers of tissue:

1. Outer covering of skin.
2. Superficial pelvic floor muscles.
   (*a*) Bulbo-cavernosus.
   (*b*) Transverse Perinei.
3. Deep pelvic floor muscle—pubo-coccygeus.

Blood Supply

The blood supply is from the pudendal arteries, branches of the internal iliac artery. Venous drainage is into the corresponding veins.

Figure 3.4
The Perineal Body

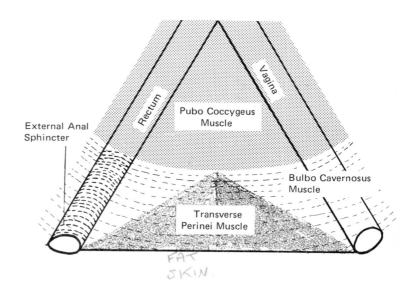

External Anal Sphincter

Rectum

Vagina

Pubo Coccygeus Muscle

Bulbo Cavernosus Muscle

Transverse Perinei Muscle

FAT
SKIN.

Lymphatic Drainage   This is into the inguinal and external iliac glands.

Perineal Branch

Nerve Supply   Nerve supply is from the perineal branch of the pudendal nerve.

Function   The function of the perineal body is to assist in the process of defaecation and childbirth. During the latter function, the structure may become overstretched or torn, and the midwife must learn how such injuries can be minimised. Trauma may result in disorders of micturition and bowel function, prolapse of the pelvic, and sometimes even of the abdominal organs.

PERINEAL TEARS

A First Degree Tear   This involves only the skin.

A Second Degree Tear   The skin and superficial muscles are involved, but a deep tear of this degree will also involve the deep muscles.

A Third Degree Tear   By far the most serious is the third degree tear. Not only skin and the perineal muscles are involved, but also the anal sphincter muscle. Suturing of torn tissues must be carried out as soon as possible after delivery and the perineal area then kept as clean and dry as possible. A third degree tear should be repaired by a skilled obstetrician and is often sutured under general anaesthesia.

Prevention of Tears   The expectant mother should be prepared for labour in the
Antenatal Period   following ways:

1. *Attention to general health* and prevention of anaemia. A healthy body is more likely to perform its functions in a satisfactory way.
2. *Health education.* A basic knowledge of the process of labour should be taught, and the mother shown how she can co-operate during the first and second stages.
3. *Psychoprophylaxis* or some other form of labour preparation should be taught.
4. *Antenatal exercises* carried out daily will improve muscle tone.
5. *Teach the use of inhalational analgesia.* It is too late to teach this when the patient is already in labour, she is not then in a receptive frame of mind.

Throughout the antenatal period, the midwife should be gaining the confidence and trust of her patient.

During Labour   1. *Prevent long first stage* as far as possible by antenatal preparation and the use of analgesic drugs given at the correct time. The patient should not be allowed to 'bear down' in the first stage of labour. This causes overstretching of muscles and also results in oedema of the cervix which prolongs the first stage even further.

2. *Skilful delivery.* In the second stage of labour (the stage of expulsion of the fetus) careful attention must be paid to delivery of the fetal head. The mother should be asked to 'pant' out the baby's head between contractions. The smallest diameters possible must be allowed to distend the vulva and perineum. This is a technique which can only be learned by practical experience during midwifery practice.

The midwife must keep her hands off the perineum. Handling is likely to cause bruising of these greatly distended tissues and bruised tissues tear more easily.

If there is a delay of more than thirty minutes in the descent of the fetal head then an obstetrician should be informed. The wise use of episiotomy (surgical incision of the perineum) and forceps delivery will prevent excessive trauma to both the perineum and the fetal head. Episiotomy must also be considered if the perineal tissues show signs of tearing. A clean incision is said to heal more readily than a ragged tear.

Once the head has been delivered the midwife must wait for the anterior shoulder to rotate and come to lie under the pubic arch. The large diameter of the shoulders is then lying in the antero-posterior diameter of the pelvis outlet where most room is available. The anterior shoulder should then be allowed to escape, after which the baby's body is taken upwards in a movement of lateral flexion over the mother's abdomen. This allows the posterior shoulder and the baby to escape through the curved birth canal without further pressure on the perineum.

A midwife who has gained the confidence and trust of her patient throughout pregnancy is more likely to have a co-operative patient who will obey instructions during the second stage of labour, thus further minimising trauma.

EPISIOTOMY

Definition
(Figure 3.5)

A surgical incision of the perineum which is carried out prior to the delivery of the infant.

Indications

To expedite delivery in the following circumstances:

1. Pre-eclampsia.
2. Eclampsia.
3. Cardiac or respiratory disease.
4. Previous operation for pelvic floor repair.
5. Maternal distress.
6. Fetal distress.
7. Cord prolapse.

To prevent excessive trauma:

1. Rigid perineum.
2. Buttonholing of perineum.
3. Previous third degree tear.
4. Prior forceps delivery.
5. Face to pubes delivery.
6. Face delivery.
7. Narrow pubic arch.

To prevent cerebral damage:

1. Slow advance of head.
2. Prematurity.
3. After coming head of the breech.

The Central Midwives Board has stated that when the necessity arises in advanced labour, and when there is no doctor present, a midwife should be allowed to infiltrate the perineum and perform an episiotomy. The Board recommends that trained midwives should have a supply of local anaesthetic when attending a woman in labour, and that the techniques of perineal infiltration and incision be taught to pupil midwives during their training period, practical experience being given where possible.

Infiltration of the Perineum

This is an aseptic procedure. 10 cm^3 of 0.5 per cent xylocaine without adrenaline is drawn up into a syringe and a number 1 needle is attached.

Between uterine contractions, two fingers are inserted into the vagina between the fetal head and the perineum. This ensures that

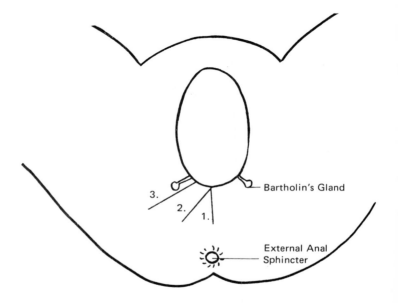

Figure 3.5
Different Types of
Episiotomy: (1) medial
(2) mediolateral, (3)
lateral

the area to be infiltrated is well distinguished and that the fetal head is protected.

Air bubbles are expelled from the syringe, the needle inserted into the perineal skin at the mid-line of the fourchette and a little xylocaine infiltrated. If the medio-lateral type of incision is to be made the needle is then passed in the direction of line 2 on Figure 3.5, xylocaine being infiltrated into the tissues as the needle is passed. The local anaesthetic will take approximately 5 min to reach its full effect.

Before making this injection:

1. The patient should be given a simple explanation of the procedure, and told that she will feel only a small pricking.
2. The patient should be asked if she has ever had a local anaesthetic before. This is because she may have had a reaction to the drug. In sensitive patients, reaction is shown by a fall in blood pressure, respirations which become distressed, and the patient may develop convulsions.

Before any injection of xylocaine is made, the piston of the syringe should be withdrawn to ensure that no blood vessels have been penetrated.

Incision of the Perineum

Three types of episiotomy are described, but the one used most commonly is the medio-lateral incision because this avoids Bartholin's gland and duct and diminishes the likelihood of involvement of the external anal sphincter.

Two fingers are placed in the vagina, as for infiltration of the perineum, and are used as before to distinguish the area and to protect the fetal head.

Long, blunt ended scissors are used, one end being passed into the vagina. The incision is started in midline and directed laterally. It is made through the perineal skin and muscles with one determined cut approximately 4 cm (1.5 in) in length. The incision should be made during a uterine contraction when the perineal tissues are thinned, so that bleeding is controlled by pressure of the fetal head.

Following this widening of the soft tissue outlet, delivery of the baby will normally occur quite easily. The wound should then be sutured by a doctor as soon as labour is completed. Every midwife should become familiar with this technique because it is so often the means of facilitating spontaneous vaginal delivery with the minimum of trauma to the mother and her infant.

Advantages:

1. Prevents overstretching of pelvic floor muscles.
2. Does not extend to involve the anus.
3. Reduces maternal exhaustion and therefore lowers the incidence of post-partum haemorrhage.
4. Reduces the risk of cerebral damage to the infant.
5. Heals more readily than a ragged tear.

Disadvantages:

1. It is a mutilation if used without good cause.
2. The scar may cause dyspareunia if not sutured correctly.
3. The resulting scar tissue may make episiotomy necessary in subsequent pregnancies.

Following Delivery

Lacerations will heal more readily and tissues regain their tone more readily if the following points are observed:

1. Prompt suturing of lacerations.
2. The wound be kept clean and dry.
3. Gentle and graduated post-natal exercises taught.
4. Early ambulation encouraged.
5. Attention paid to general health.
6. Prevention or treatment of anaemia.
7. Non-absorbent sutures removed alternately on sixth and seventh days.

Should a third degree tear have been sustained, an aperient with a lubricant action is given daily until the sutures are removed. Vulval toilet should be carried out if the patient is confined to bed, otherwise saline baths have both a soothing and healing effect.

Pain due to a perineal wound can be relieved by the administration of a drug containing a concentrate of proteolytic enzymes. This drug acts upon the soft fibrin deposits in the tissues, thus reducing inflammation and oedema. Two tablets of the drug are given four times a day for forty-eight hours, and give rapid relief from symptoms.

What are the causes of lacerations of the perineum during delivery? Describe how you would attempt to avoid a perineal tear during a normal vertex delivery.

Describe the vagina and perineum. How may injuries to these structures be minimised during labour and delivery?

Describe the perineal body. How may this be damaged in labour and what steps can be taken to minimise this danger?

What are the indications for episiotomy? When should a midwife undertake this procedure? Describe the technique she might employ.

What anatomical structures are incised during the procedure of episiotomy? What are the advantages and disadvantages of this procedure?

4
The Bladder and Urethra

THE BLADDER

Situation

The bladder lies in the true pelvis with its base resting on the upper half of the vagina and the apex pointing towards the symphysis pubis.

Shape

It is like a pyramid when empty but becomes globular as it fills with urine.

Size

About 420 cm³ (14 fl oz) of urine can be contained comfortably, but the bladder is capable of very great distension.

Gross Structure
(Figure 4.1)

There is:

1. A base: known as the **trigone**.
2. An apex: pointing towards the symphysis pubis.
3. A neck: the point where the urethra enters.

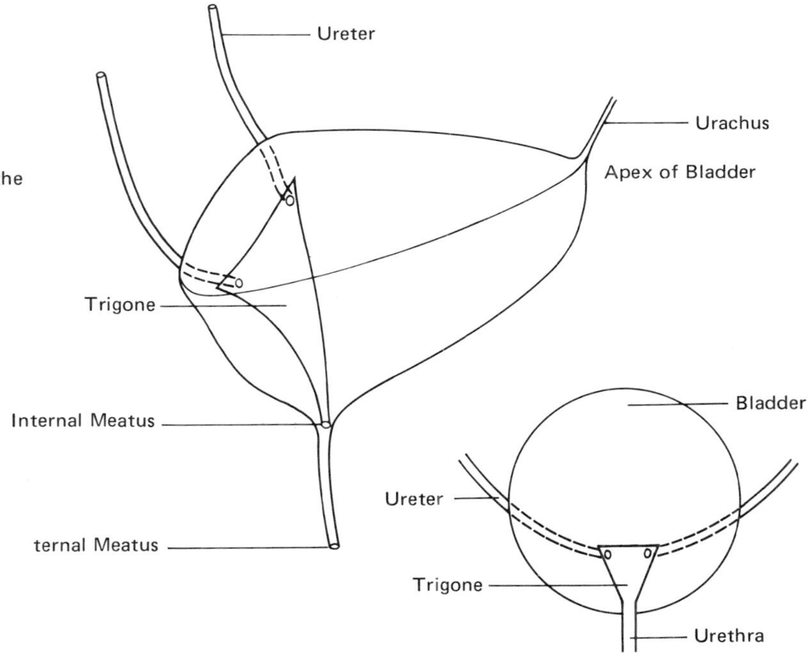

Figure 4.1
Gross Structure of the
Bladder

Microscopic Structure
(excluding the trigone)

Transitional epithelium forms the lining and is arranged in folds, the rugae, to allow for expansion.
Connective tissue.
Muscle coat is arranged in three layers:

1. Inner longitudinal fibres. ⎫
2. Middle circular fibres.   ⎬ known as **detrusor muscle.**
3. Outer longitudinal fibres. ⎭

    Peritoneum covers the roof of the bladder and forms part of the utero-vesical pouch.

The Trigone
(Figure 4.2)

This forms a triangular shape, each side of the triangle being 2.5 cm (0.75 in) in length. Entering obliquely at each upper angle are the ureters which pass about 2 cm (1 in) through the bladder wall. The urethra leaves from the third angle of the triangle.

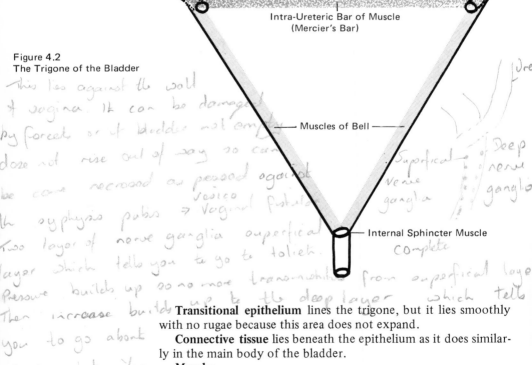

Intra-Ureteric Bar of Muscle
(Mercier's Bar)

Figure 4.2
The Trigone of the Bladder

— Muscles of Bell —

— Internal Sphincter Muscle

    Transitional epithelium lines the trigone, but it lies smoothly with no rugae because this area does not expand.
    Connective tissue lies beneath the epithelium as it does similarly in the main body of the bladder.
    Muscle:

1. *Mercier's bar,* or intra-ureteric bar, is the muscle lying between the ureteric orifices.
2. *Bell's muscles* extend downwards at each side of the trigone. They extend between the ureteric orifice and the internal meatus of the urethra.

Handwritten notes:

This lies against the wall of vagina. It can be damaged by forceps or if bladder not emptied does not rise out of way so can be caused necrosed or pressed against the symphysis pubis → vaginal fistula. Two layer of nerve ganglia superficial layer which tells you to go to toilet. Pressure builds up so no more ... meanwhile from superficial layer ... up to the deep layer which tells. Then increase builds up to deep layer which tells you to go about 1½ hr later. You have to go to toilet if this layer damaged it cannot be replaced.

Ureter

Deep nerve ganglion

Superficial } nerve
Vena   } ganglia

complete

Blood Supply	Inferior and superior vesical arteries. Drainage by the vesical veins.
Lymphatic Drainage	Drainage into the external iliac glands.
Nerve Supply	Sympathetic and parasympathetic nerves from the Lee Frankenhauser plexus.
Supports	*Two lateral ligaments* from the side walls of the bladder to the side walls of the pelvis.
	Two pubo-vesical ligaments from the neck of the bladder to the symphysis pubis.
	The urachus extends from the apex of the bladder to the umbilicus.
Function	To store urine until it can be voided.
Relations	*Anterior*: the symphysis pubis.
	Posterior: upper half of the vagina. The cervix.
	Superior: utero-vesical pouch. Body of the uterus.
	Inferior: the urethra, embedded in the anterior vaginal wall.
	Lateral: the pelvic floor muscles.

THE URETHRA

Situation	The urethra extends from the apex of the trigone to the external meatus in the vestibule of the vulva and is embedded in the anterior vaginal wall.
Shape	Tubular, containing blind crypts.
Size	In the female it is 4 cm (1.5 in) long, but capable of elongating as it does during labour.
Gross Structure	*Internal meatus* where it meets the neck of the bladder.
	External meatus: the opening in the vestibule.
	Urethral crypts: small, blind ducts open from the wall of the urethra. The lowest ones at each side turn downwards and open on each side of the urethral orifice. These are known as Skene's ducts.
Microscopic Structure	*Stratified epithelium* lines the lower half of the urethra.
	Transitional epithelium lines the upper half.
	Connective tissue lies beneath the epithelium.
	Muscle coat is arranged in two layers:

1. Inner layer of longitudinal fibres.
2. Outer layer of longitudinal fibres.

The muscle is thickened around the internal meatus to form the *internal sphincter muscle.* The external meatus is surrounded by the *membranous sphincter.* The urethra needs no outer protective coat because it is embedded in the anterior wall of the vagina.

Blood Supply

Inferior vesical artery and the pudendal artery. Venous drainage by corresponding veins.

Lymphatic Drainage

Drainage into the internal iliac glands.

Nerve Supply

Sympathetic nerves to the internal sphincter. The membranous sphincter is under control of the will and is supplied by the pudendal nerve.

Supports

Support is given by the anterior vaginal wall and the pelvic floor muscles.

Function

It forms a canal through which urine can be eliminated from the body.

PHYSIOLOGY OF MICTURITION

The sensation of a full bladder is conveyed to the brain by sensory sympathetic nerves. Then, at a suitable time:

1. Voluntary nerves relax the membranous sphincter;
2. Sympathetic nerves relax the internal sphincter;
3. Parasympathetic nerves cause the detrusor muscles to contract, and this results in the internal meatus being pulled open by Bell's muscle;
4. Intra-abdominal pressure is then increased and urine is passed with a 'bearing down' movement.

URINARY DISORDERS

Because of the proximity of the uterus, cervix, and vagina to the bladder and urethra their functions are correlated during childbearing and childbirth. Disorders of micturition are therefore fairly common complaints during pregnancy, labour, and the puerperium.

In Pregnancy
Increased Frequency

In the first twelve weeks of pregnancy, while the enlarging uterus is still a pelvic organ, the bladder requires to be emptied at more frequent intervals because there is less room for it to expand. This type of increased frequency is said to be **physiological**. During the last four weeks of pregnancy when the fetal head lies in the pelvis there is a recurrence of increased frequency.

In the middle weeks of pregnancy, increased frequency arising in association with dysuria is due to **urinary infection**. This commonly arises between the sixteenth and twenty-fourth weeks of pregnancy, and is a difficult condition to cure at this time. It may recur throughout pregnancy and the puerperium. About 2 per cent of pregnant women are affected.

Acute Retention

This is a rare complication of pregnancy but sometimes occurs at about the twelfth week of gestation if the uterus is retroverted. The uterus cannot rise out of the pelvis beyond the hollow of the sacrum if the bladder is full and the uterus therefore becomes impacted. This is a vicious circle; the uterus cannot rise out of the pelvis until the bladder is emptied, but the bladder cannot be spontaneously emptied because it is nipped between the symphysis pubis and the enlarged uterus. The treatment lies in passing a urinary catheter and slowly draining the bladder after which there are rarely any further complications.

Incontinence

Urine is sometimes passed involuntarily towards the end of pregnancy if the fetal head is deeply engaged in the pelvis. Small amounts of urine may be passed if the patient coughs, sneezes, or laughs. Incontinence of urine should not be confused with early rupture of membranes.

In Labour
Increased Frequency

This occurs most frequently as a result of occipito-posterior position. Pressure on the sacral plexus of nerves causes excess stimulation of the nerves to the bladder. Very often the patient has a desire to micturate but cannot actually do so.

Acute Retention

Pressure on the sacral plexus of nerves may conversely cause a lack of stimulus to the bladder. In addition, the urethra stretches from 4 cm (1.5 in) in length to something like 15 or 18 cm (6 or 7 in) during labour, thus almost occluding the lumen. This makes not only micturition but also catheterisation very difficult if the procedure is delayed until labour is well advanced.

Incontinence

If the bladder is not emptied at the end of the first stage of labour, there is a dribbling of urine with each expulsive contraction during the second stage. An attempt should be made to empty the bladder by catheterisation.

A full bladder causes delay in the first and second stages of labour by preventing good uterine contractions. Bruising of a full bladder can occur during descent of the fetal head because the bladder is then nipped between the head and the symphysis pubis. Similar bruising of the urethra occurs in addition to overstretching. In the third stage of labour uterine contractions are also inhibited by a full bladder, causing delay in separation or descent of the placenta and also post-partum haemorrhage.

In the Puerperium
Increased Frequency

During the first forty-eight hours of the puerperium, an excessive amount of urine is secreted. Increased frequency at this time is therefore **physiological**. As in pregnancy, increased frequency may also be due to **infection**. It may also occur as a result of **lax muscle tone**.

Acute Retention

This may be caused by:

1. *Posture*: when the patient is confined to bed and must use a bed-pan; she is not accustomed to this position for micturition.
2. *Embarrassment*: when other people are nearby.
3. *Fear of pain*: especially when the perineum has been sutured or delivery has been difficult.
4. *Insufficient stimulus*: when there has been pressure on the bladder during labour and delivery, causing a diminution of nerve stimulus.
5. *Lax muscle tone*: this may result from over-distension of the bladder.

During the lying-in period the abdomen should be palpated daily in order to diagnose retention of urine. Sometimes the bladder is incompletely emptied on micturition and urine then accumulates. This can result in urinary infection because of the stasis of urine and also in subinvolution of the uterus with the possibility of post-partum haemorrhage, because the uterus cannot contract effectively when the bladder is full.

Incontinence

True incontinence is rarely seen in this country today as a complication of obstetrics. It results from a major degree of trauma such as a vesico-vaginal fistula. It might occur if the patient were unconscious, but a self-retaining catheter would then be passed *because* the patient was unconscious.

Much more commonly, the complication known as **stress incontinence** is seen. It is more common in the multigravida, and is the result of lax pelvic floor muscles and weakened sphincters.

Describe the anatomy of the female bladder and urethra. Why is it important that a midwife should have this knowledge?

Describe the urethra. Discuss the obstetric indications for catheterisation of the bladder.

Describe the urethra and give its relations. Under what conditions may retention of urine occur during pregnancy, labour, and the puerperium?

Describe the female bladder and urethra. How may these structures be affected by pregnancy and labour?

Describe the urinary bladder. What disturbances of micturition may occur during pregnancy, labour, and the puerperium?

Describe the anatomy of the bladder. How may urinary infections be avoided in pregnancy, labour, and the puerperium?

5

The External Genital Organs

The external genital organs of the female are known collectively as the **vulva** and include the following structures (Figure 5.1).

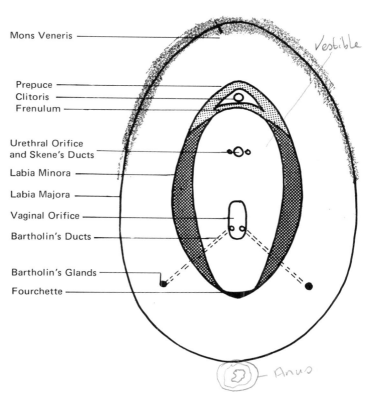

Figure 5.1
The External Genital
Organs

Mons Veneris
Vestible
Prepuce
Clitoris
Frenulum
Urethral Orifice and Skene's Ducts
Labia Minora
Labia Majora
Vaginal Orifice
Bartholin's Ducts
Bartholin's Glands
Fourchette
Anus

The Mons Veneris

A pad of fatty tissue, covered by skin, which lies over the symphysis pubis. After puberty, a growth of hair develops on it.

Labia Majora

Two large rounded folds of fatty tissue covered by skin which meet anteriorly at the mons veneris. As they pass backwards towards the anus they become flatter and merge into the perineal body. The terminal portions of the round ligaments are inserted into the fatty tissue. The inner aspects of the labia are smooth and contain numerous sweat and sebaceous glands while their outer aspects, after puberty, are covered with hair.

Labia Minora

Two smaller folds of pink skin lying longitudinally within the labia majora. They are smooth, having no covering of hair but do contain a few sweat and sebaceous glands. The area they enclose is known as the **vestibule**. Each labium minus divides into two folds anteriorly. The upper folds surround the **clitoris** and unite to form the **prepuce**. The two lower folds are attached to the under surface of the clitoris and are known as the **frenulum**. Posteriorly, the labia minora unite forming a thin fold of skin, the **fourchette**, which is torn when a first degree perineal tear is sustained during delivery.

The Clitoris

A small, extremely sensitive, erectile structure, situated, as previously explained, within the folds of the prepuce and frenulum. It is composed of two bodies, the **corpora cavernosa**, which lie side by side and extend backwards to be attached to the periosteum of the bodies of the pubic bones. The clitoris is a structure which may be compared with the male penis, but unlike the penis does not transmit the urethra. In some areas of Africa the female circumcision rite (at which the clitoris is excised) was practised until quite recently. The 'operation' leaves a great deal of scarring of the vulva which will almost certainly rupture during delivery of the fetal head, and therefore midwives working in largely immigrant areas should observe their patients carefully for this type of trauma.

The Vestibule

In order to observe the vestibule, the folds of the labia must be separated to bring it into view. There are six openings into it:

The Urethral Meatus

Known also as the **external orifice** of the urethra, it lies 2.5 cm below the clitoris.

Two Skene's Ducts

The openings of Skene's tubules which run parallel with the urethra for about 6 mm, and then open one on each side of the urethral orifice.

The Vaginal Orifice

Also known as **introitus** which occupies the lower two thirds of the vestibule. In the virgin this is covered by the hymen, a thin perforated membrane through which the menstrual flow can pass. The hymen is ruptured following intercourse and further laceration occurs during childbirth, the remaining tags of skin being known as **carunculae myrtiformes**.

Two Bartholin's Ducts

The openings of Bartholin's glands. The glands lie on each side of the vagina, resting on the triangular ligaments. About the size and shape of haricot beans, they are composed of racemose glands and secrete mucus which keeps the external genitals moist. The ducts open outside the hymen.

Blood Supply

The pudendal arteries, branches of the femoral artery, supply the external genitals. Venous drainage is by the corresponding veins.

Lymphatic Drainage

Drainage is into the inguinal glands and some drainage is directly into the external iliac glands. _— Block on these nerves_

Nerve Supply

Branches of the pudendal nerve and the perineal nerve.

The vulva becomes very distended towards the end of the first stage of labour and even more so during the second stage when the fetal head is descending quite rapidly. A practical knowledge of the basic anatomy of these parts is therefore essential in order that the midwife can carry out such procedures as catheterisation of the bladder and episiotomy, with the maximum of efficiency and minimum of trauma to her patient.

COLLECTION OF URINE SPECIMENS

Because of the proximity of the urethral, vaginal and rectal orifices, bacillus coli, normal inhabitants of the rectum, have easy access to the urethra. The organisms flourish on blood from menstrual loss or on the lochia. All female children should therefore be taught the importance of correct rectal and perineal cleansing, i.e. cleansing in an anterior-posterior direction. Such instruction should be reinforced during the ante- and post-natal periods. Cystitis is said to occur in about 2 per cent of women, sometimes being asymptomatic.

When the laboratory is asked to test a specimen of urine for culture and deposits it is now more usual to collect a clean (i.e. midstream) specimen rather than a catheter specimen because of the risk of infecting the urinary tract when a catheter is introduced into the bladder.

Midstream Specimen
Technique

A tray containing the following equipment is required:

1 bowl of tap water
1 bowl of sterile swabs
1 sterile jug
1 urine specimen bottle
1 receiver for used swabs

Most patients are capable of carrying out this procedure themselves and are given instructions such as these. The main objective is to prevent contamination of the urine.

1. To remove clothing from below the waist.
2. To wash and dry the hands.
3. Stand astride toilet.
4. The labia should be separated with thumb and forefinger of left hand.
5. Using the right hand and separate swabs for each movement, to swab the inner sides of the right and then the left labium. The movement should start at the front and move backwards

towards the rectum. Another swab is then used to cleanse the central area, again moving from the front towards the rectum.

6. Urine is then passed into the lavatory and, after a little has been voided, about 60 ml in midstream should be collected in the sterile jug, or the specimen bottle filled directly.

If the patient has a vaginal discharge then the midwife should carry out this procedure for her, plugging the vagina with a large swab before asking the patient to pass urine. This plug must be removed immediately following the procedure. The specimen of urine in the sterile jug is then transferred into the specimen bottle, labelled and sent with the request form to the laboratory.

Catheter Specimen

There are a few occasions when of necessity a catheter must be passed into the bladder because the patient cannot pass urine voluntarily. The following are occasions when a catheter is used.

1. *Antenatal period.* An incarcerated, retroverted, pregnant uterus which cannot rise out of the pelvis and which, therefore, interferes with bladder function.

2. *In labour.* During the first or second stages of labour, the descending fetal head may interfere with bladder function. If the bladder is not emptied trauma may occur. A full bladder in the third stage of labour should always be emptied, as it affects uterine action and can cause post-partum haemorrhage.

3. *In the puerperium.* First, acute retention of urine is less common when the early ambulation of patients is practised, but it does occur from time to time.

Second, retention with overflow is another occasional complication, this being a condition in which the bladder is not emptied when the patient urinates: the amount of residual urine is therefore increased daily.

Third, true incontinence occurs, rarely, as a result of prolonged and difficult labour, and as a consequence of trauma the urine is blood-stained. In this condition a self-retaining catheter should be inserted and left in situ at least until the urine is clear. Catheterisation should never be carried out unless it is absolutely necessary, and when this necessity does arise it should be a sterile procedure, undertaken with scrupulous care.

Technique

A sterile trolley with the following equipment is required:

1 bowl of sterile swabs
1 bowl of sterile lotion
2 urinary catheters } usually packed in container by CSSD
1 pair sterile gloves
3 sterile towels

A good light is required.

The procedure is explained to the patient and her bed is screened to give privacy. She is asked to lie on her back with her knees drawn up and flexed. A blanket is placed across her chest to keep her warm. The nurse washes her hands, puts on sterile gloves and drapes the patient's thighs and abdomen with the three sterile towels.

The labia are swabbed in the same way as described for the technique of obtaining a midstream specimen, but the right hand should be kept sterile and the left hand used for swabbing. The left hand is used to separate the labia and the urethral orifice is exposed. The right hand is used to insert the catheter. Should the catheter be brought into contact with any part of the genitalia before being inserted into the urethra it must be discarded and another catheter substituted.

If catheterisation is being performed during labour it will be found necessary to insert a greater length of catheter than when a similar procedure is undertaken in the ante- or post-natal periods.

The bladder is slowly emptied and then the catheter withdrawn, unless orders for the insertion of a self-retaining catheter have been given. The patient is left dry and comfortable. A specimen of the urine is sent to the laboratory with a request for investigations.

SPECIMEN
QUESTIONS

Describe the vulva. What pathological conditions of the vulva may occur during pregnancy?

Describe the anatomy of the external female genital organs. How would you obtain a specimen of urine for laboratory investigations?

Describe the anatomy of the external female genital organs. Of what importance is this knowledge (a) to all women (b) to a midwife.

Describe how you would instruct a patient (a) to collect a midstream specimen of urine (b) to perform personal vulval and perineal toilet. Give reasons for your instructions.

6
The Vagina

Situation

The vagina is a canal which extends from the vulva to the uterus. It runs upwards and backwards parallel to the plane of the pelvic brim.

Shape

Its shape is that of a potential tube, the walls normally lying in close contact with each other, but becoming easily separated during intercourse or by the products of conception.

Size

Because the cervix enters the vagina at right angles, the posterior vaginal wall is longer than that of the anterior when the uterus is anteverted. The anterior wall is approximately 7.5 cm (3 in) long and the posterior 11.5 cm (4.5 in). Should the uterus be retroverted then these measurements will be reversed.

Gross Structure

Four fornices are formed where the cervix projects into the vagina. These are named **anterior, posterior,** or **lateral** according to their position: the posterior fornix is the largest. At the external orifice of the vagina, the **hymen** covers the opening, or, if the hymen has been ruptured, the **carunculae myrtiformes** are found instead.

Microscopic Structure

Squamous epithelium is a type of modified skin and forms the vaginal lining.

> *Vascular connective tissue.*
> *Muscle coat* is arranged in two layers:
> (*a*) inner circular fibres
> (*b*) outer longitudinal fibres

Although this muscle coat is rather thin, it is nevertheless very strong.

Fascia: loose connective tissue which is part of the pelvic cellular tissue.

The walls of the vagina do not lie smoothly but fall into transverse folds, *the rugae,* which allows for distension. In a patient who has borne several children, the rugae have been stretched several times, and are therefore not as obvious on inspection.

Blood Supply

Vaginal, uterine, haemorrhoidal, inferior vesical, and pudendal branches of the internal iliac artery. Venous drainage is by corresponding vessels.

Lymphatic Drainage   Lymphatic drainage is into the inguinal, internal iliac, and sacral glands.

Nerve Supply   Sympathetic and parasympathetic nerves from the Lee Frankenhauser plexus. _Bladder Vaginal Rectum._

Relations
(Figure 6.1)

1. *Anterior*: Base of bladder rests on upper half of vagina. Urethra is embedded in the lower half.
2. *Posterior*: (*a*) pouch of Douglas—superiorly, (*b*) rectum—centrally, (*c*) perineal body—inferiorly.
3. *Lateral*: Pubococcygeus muscle below. Pelvic fascia containing ureter above.
4. *Inferior*: Structures of the vulva.
5. *Superior*: The cervix.

Functions

1. Entrance for spermatozoa.   _Kill weaker spermatozoa_
2. Exit for products of conception. ← _Products of conception_
3. Helps to support the uterus.
4. Helps to prevent infection.

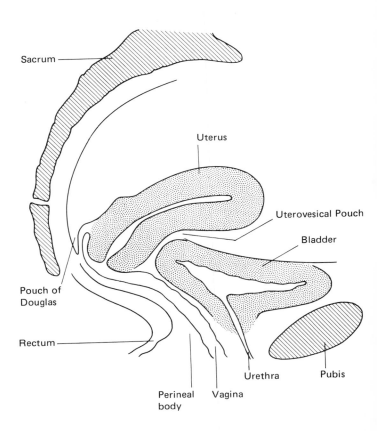

Figure 6.1
Relation of the Pelvic
Organs (cross section
through pelvis)

Sacrum

Uterus

Uterovesical Pouch

Bladder

Pouch of
Douglas

Rectum

Urethra

Pubis

Perineal
body

Vagina

PH = 4·5

There is an acid medium in the vagina provided by Doderlein's bacilli which are normal inhabitants; this medium therefore destroys pathogenic organisms. If these bacilli are absent or reduced in number, the acidity of the vagina is altered resulting in a consequent vaginitis. Expectant mothers should therefore be advised not to use antiseptic preparations in their bath or for vulval and vaginal toilet purposes except under medical supervision.

The midwife must remember that if lacerations of the vaginal wall occur during delivery, or if the muscles are overstretched, other structures are likely to be affected (the urethra and bladder being most commonly involved) resulting in disorders of micturition.

VAGINAL DISCHARGES ASSOCIATED WITH PREGNANCY

Physiological

A clear inoffensive discharge, just a little heavier than usual, is quite normal during pregnancy and is brought about by the extra hormonal activity. No treatment is necessary except for advising more frequent vulval hygiene and changes of underclothing.

Moniliasis

This is a fungus infection caused by Candida albicans. White curdy patches can be seen on the vaginal walls and there is a greyish white staining of pads and underclothes. It causes extreme irritation, and is often found in association with diabetes as well as pregnancy.

Diagnosis is easy as the clinical appearance is distinctive, but a vaginal swab is sent to the laboratory for microscopic examination.

The treatment ordered is a course of Nystatin pessaries. One should be inserted into the vagina both night and morning for one to two weeks depending upon the severity of the condition. Subsequently, one is inserted each night until thirty-five pessaries have been used. Alternatively, the vagina should be swabbed with a sodium bicarbonate solution two or three times a week and then painted with 0.5 per cent gentian violet solution.

The disease can be transmitted to the male partner and he should therefore be given a course of oral Nystatin.

Should the infection be transmitted to the fetus during delivery, a troublesome thrush develops. It is therefore essential that the mother's infection should be cleared before delivery is imminent, or the baby will require treatment for 'sticky' eyes, or oral thrush.

Trichomoniasis

The infection caused by the protozoa, Trichomonas vaginalis, appears as a greenish, yellow, frothy, watery discharge, and has a distinctive odour. The patient complains of acute irritation and inflammation of the genital area.

Diagnosis is made by accurate history-taking and laboratory examination of the vaginal discharge. As the condition is sometimes associated with gonorrhoea, this condition must be excluded.

Treatment for trichomoniasis is with oral Flagyl. One tablet is taken three times a day for one week. Alternatively, Stovarsol pessaries can be used, two being inserted into the vagina each night for two weeks. This is less favoured during pregnancy because Stovarsol is an arsenic preparation.

The husband is likely to be infected and he should also be given a course of oral Flagyl.

Following treatment of both moniliasis and trichomoniasis, vaginal swabs should be cultured to ensure that the infection has cleared.

Gonorrhoea

Infection is transmitted by sexual intercourse and the organism is the gonococcus. The patient complains of a greenish, offensive, pus-like discharge causing the genital area to be inflamed and oedematous. It is accompanied by urethritis and dysuria and it is possible to milk pus from Skene's tubules. A Bartholin's abscess may be present.

Gonorrhoea is confirmed by examination of the vaginal discharge in the laboratory. The patient is referred to the venereal disease clinic and is treated by large doses of the most appropriate antibiotic. The patient's husband should also receive treatment.

If gonorrhoea is not treated, there is a likelihood of the infection spreading through the genital tract and causing a generalised pelvic infection. Early in pregnancy the patient may abort or, later, the baby may be stillborn. If the baby is born alive he must be treated for gonococcal infection immediately; his eyes are likely to be infected, a condition which could result in subsequent blindness.

Blood

If blood is passed per vaginam at any stage of pregnancy, the patient should seek medical advice at once. Early in pregnancy it may signify an impending abortion and, after the twenty-eighth week, is a possible sign of early placental separation. It is important that the actual cause be found as soon as possible as the life of both mother and baby may be in danger.

VAGINAL EXAMINATIONS

Antenatal

At the patient's first visit to the antenatal clinic the doctor will probably perform a vaginal examination for the following reasons:

1. To confirm pregnancy.
2. To exclude abnormality of the pelvic organs.
3. To assess the size of the pelvis.

A further examination is made at about the thirty-sixth week of pregnancy:

1. To exclude later abnormalities of the pelvic organs.
2. To re-assess the size of the pelvic brim and cavity if the fetal head is not engaged.
3. To assess the size of the pelvis in relation to the fetal head and to ensure that the head is able to pass through the pelvis.
4. To ensure that the pelvic outlet is adequate.

In Labour

The midwife may perform vaginal examinations during labour *unless*:

1. The patient has a history of ante-partum haemorrhage.
2. The patient has been admitted for 'trial of labour'.
3. Labour is in any way not normal.

Indications for Vaginal Examination

1. To determine the onset of labour.
2. To determine the presentation or engagement if there is any doubt.
3. To exclude cord prolapse when the membranes rupture early.
4. To determine dilatation of the cervix before giving rectal suppositories to a multigravida.
5. To determine dilatation of the cervix before giving analgesic drugs.
6. To confirm full dilatation of the cervix when there is any doubt.

Technique

1. Explain the procedure to patient.
2. Ask patient to empty bladder.
3. Examine the abdomen by:
   (*a*) Inspection.
   (*b*) Palpation.
   (*c*) Auscultation of fetal heart.
4. Midwife puts on mask and rubber gloves.
5. Vulval toilet is performed, the right hand being kept 'clean'.
6. Index and middle finger of right hand are used to make the examination.

Observations to Record

1. *External genitalia*: oedema, varicose veins, warts, perineal scars.
2. *Condition of vagina*: it should be warm and be easily distended with the fingers. A hot vagina indicates that the patient is pyrexial. A tight vagina indicates a tense patient. Any vaginal discharge is noted.
3. *The cervix*: note whether the cervix is thin or thick, whether soft or rigid, and whether well applied to the fetal head.
4. *Dilatation of the os*: this is usually assessed by the number of finger breadths that the os will admit.
5. *Membranes*: record whether these are bulging, intact, or ruptured.

6. *Presentation*:
    (*a*) ensure that head is presenting,
    (*b*) assess whether it is above or below at the level of the ischial spines,
    (*c*) confirm position by finding sutures and fontanelles and relating them to maternal pelvis,
    (*d*) note the degree of moulding or caput formation.
7. *Pelvic outlet*: the ischial spines should be palpated and the size of the pubic arch estimated.

When the fingers are withdrawn from the vagina they should be examined for meconium staining. These observations should be recorded on the patient's notes and illustrated with a diagram. (*See* Figure 6.2.)

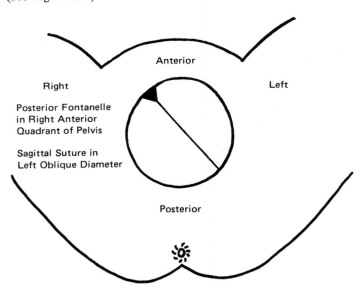

Figure 6.2
Vaginal Examination.
Right Occipito Anterior
Position of Fetus

Post-natal

Before the patient is discharged home and then six weeks after delivery a vaginal examination is made by the doctor to ensure:

1. That the uterus is anteverted, anteflexed, and of normal size.
2. That the cervix has re-formed and that the external os is only a slit-like aperture.
3. That the cervix is healthy. It is examined with a light and a speculum to exclude cervical erosions, and a cervical smear is sent to the cytology technician.
4. That vaginal and perineal lacerations have all healed.
5. Tone of the pelvic floor muscles.

Describe the vagina. What information may be obtained from a
vaginal examination during labour?

Describe the vagina. With what other organs does it come in contact? What information can be gained from a vaginal examination
during labour?

Describe the anatomical relations of the vagina. Indicate their
importance in midwifery.

Describe the vagina and perineum. How may injuries to these
structures be minimised during labour and delivery?

Describe the vagina and its anatomical relations. What are the
causes of vaginal bleeding during pregnancy?

List the indications for vaginal examination:
(a) in pregnancy
(b) at the post-natal examination.

7
The Cervix

Situation

The cervix forms the lower third of the uterus and enters the vagina at right angles. It is sometimes called the 'neck' of the uterus.

Shape

The cervical canal is fusiform and the cervix as a whole tends to be barrel-shaped.

Size

Approximately 2.5 cm (1 in) long.

Gross Structure
(Figure 7.1)

The supra-vaginal cervix lies above and outside the vagina. The infra-vaginal cervix is the portion lying within the vagina. The internal os opens into the cavity of the uterus. The external os opens into the vagina. The cervical canal lies between the internal and external os.

Figure 7.1
Gross Structure of the
Cervix

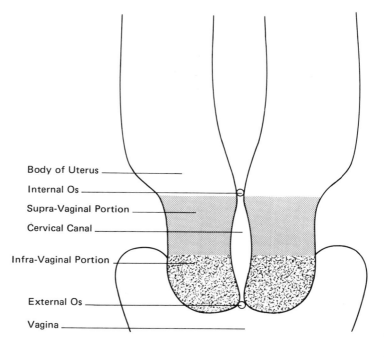

Body of Uterus

Internal Os

Supra-Vaginal Portion

Cervical Canal

Infra-Vaginal Portion

External Os

Vagina

Microscopic Structure

There are three layers of tissue.

A lining of endometrium which contains many racemose glands, some cells being ciliated. It is arranged in folds giving a tree like appearance, the *arbor vitae*. The cervical endometrium differs from that of the body of the uterus and plays no part in menstruation.

The muscle coat is arranged in two layers:

1. An inner layer of circular fibres which are thickly arranged and allow the cervix to dilate during labour.
2. An outer layer of longitudinal fibres which extend from the body of the uterus. These fibres cause the cervix to shorten during labour.

Peritoneum covers that part of the cervix which lies anteriorly and posteriorly above the vagina, with the exception of that area of cervix lying in contact with the base of the bladder.

Blood Supply

The blood is supplied through the uterine arteries, and venous drainage is through the uterine veins.

Lymphatic Drainage

The lymphatic drainage is into the internal iliac and sacral glands.

Nerve Supply

Sympathetic and parasympathetic nerves from the Lee Frankenhauser plexus.

Supports

1. *The cardinal ligament*: extending from the cervix to the lateral walls of the pelvis.
2. *Pubocervical ligaments*: running forwards from the cervix to the pubic bones.
3. *Uterosacral ligaments*: extending from the cervix and passing backwards to the sacrum.

Functions

1. It helps to prevent infection entering the uterus.
2. It dilates and withdraws during labour to enable vaginal delivery of the fetus and placenta.
3. Following delivery, the cervix returns almost to its non-pregnant state.

Relations

1. *Anterior*: the uterovesical pouch of peritoneum and the bladder.
2. *Posterior*: the pouch of Douglas and the rectum.
3. *Lateral*: the broad ligament and the ureters which are crossed by the uterine arteries.

This description is of the non-pregnant cervix. Certain changes occur during pregnancy, labour, and the puerperium.

In Pregnancy

The cervix has a richer blood supply and, therefore, becomes softer and more blue in colour. The cervical glands secrete more mucus and a plug of this mucoid material, the **operculum**, fills the

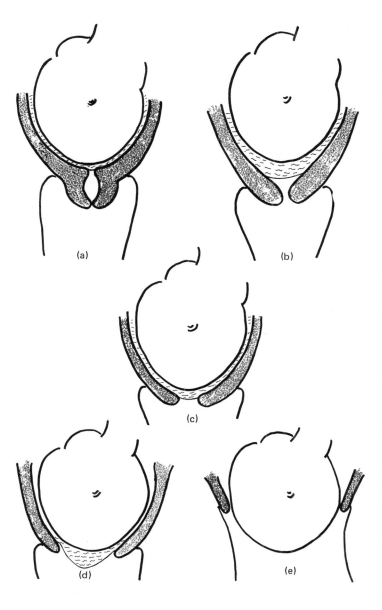

Figure 7.2
Dilatation of the Cervix in
Labour: (a) before onset of
labour (b) a 'ripe' cervix is
shorter; dilatation of
internal os has begun (c)
cervix is taken up, some
dilatation has occurred
(d) half dilatation (e) full
dilatation

cervical canal and helps to prevent infection of the genital tract.
Towards the end of pregnancy the cervix feels very much softer
and the internal os begins to dilate. This is known as 'ripening' of
the cervix.

In Labour
(Figure 7.2)

As the fetal head is pushed downwards so the internal os dilates
making the cervix funnel-shaped. The longitudinal fibres from the

body of the uterus contract and retract and pull upwards, thus reducing the length of the cervix. With each uterine contraction the cervix continues to withdraw and then the external os commences to dilate. When the cervix has opened widely enough to allow the fetal head to pass through, it is said to be 'fully dilated' and this marks the end of the first stage of labour.

Following Delivery

The cervix begins to close and return to its non-pregnant state. At the post-natal examination six weeks after the birth of the baby the cervix should have re-formed with an internal and external os and the cervical canal between them. The external os never again completely closes but becomes a slit-like aperture which is large enough to admit a finger tip. This is known as a **'multip's os'**.

Post-natal Examination

Cervical erosions, small ulcers of the cervix, often occur as a result of childbirth and these give rise to an excessive and uncomfortable vaginal discharge. At the post-natal examination the cervix should therefore be carefully examined—this is best done by using a speculum and a good light. If an erosion is seen, then a further six-week period is allowed to elapse during which time it is hoped that the erosion will heal spontaneously.

If it has not healed within this period then the patient should be referred to the gynaecology clinic for cervical cauterisation. This should clear the vaginal discharge and prevent subsequent infertility arising from this cause.

Cervical Cytology

Whenever circumstances permit, a cervical smear should be taken at the post-natal examination. Carcinoma of the cervix is really beyond the bounds of this book but because it is one of the commonest sites of cancer in women, and the midwife can play a part in its effective treatment, it must be mentioned.

Incidence

It mostly affects multiparous women between 25 and 55 years of age, and is said to have a higher incidence in those who began sexual activity at an early age and in those women classified as belonging to social groups 4 and 5. It is believed to occur less commonly in Jewish women and in those whose husbands have been circumcised. It rarely occurs in virgins.

Symptoms

Often take 15 years to become apparent, when it is too late for effective treatment. Symptoms include vaginal bleeding between periods, post-coital bleeding and post-menopausal bleeding. In the later stages a hard ulcer is visible.

Diagnosis

The condition can be diagnosed in its preinvasive stage by examination of cells scraped from around the external cervical os. If such a diagnosis is made and the cervix treated by cone biopsy or cryosurgery the prognosis is excellent.

Regular screening of all mature women should therefore be carried out. If patients attending ante-natal, post-natal or family planning clinics have not had a cervical cytology test within the last two years, the midwife should bring this to the attention of the doctor. The test takes only a few minutes to perform and might well be the means of saving the patient's life and preserving the happiness of her husband and children.

SPECIMEN
QUESTIONS

Describe the anatomy of the cervix uteri. What changes occur in it during pregnancy and labour?

Describe the anatomy of the cervix and the changes which take place during the first stage of labour.

Describe the cervix uteri and the way in which it opens during the first stage of labour.

Describe the changes that take place in the cervix during pregnancy and normal labour.

8
The Uterus

Situation

The uterus lies in the true pelvis in an anteverted and anteflexed position. The body of the uterus lies above the bladder.

Shape

Resembles that of an English pear.

Size

7.5 cm (3 in) long, 5 cm (2 in) wide, 2.5 cm (1 in) thick. The weight is approximately 57 g.

Gross Structure
(Figure 8.1)

These areas are described:

1. *The cervix*: this forms the lower third of the uterus and has previously been described in detail.
2. *The isthmus*: is the narrowed constriction about 7 mm thick lying immediately above the cervix.
3. *The cornua*: are the areas where the Fallopian tubes are inserted.

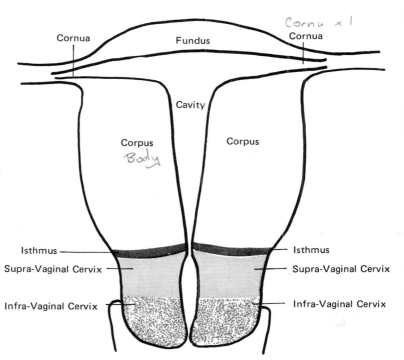

Figure 8.1
Gross Structure of the Uterus

4. *The fundus*: is the portion lying between and above the cornua.
5. *The cavity*: is the triangular shaped hollow in the centre of the organ.
6. *The corpus*: or body forms the upper two thirds of the uterus and is the whole of that area lying above the cervix.

Microscopic Structure

There are three layers of tissue.

Endometrium. A mucous membrane which lines the cavity of the uterus. The appearance of this lining varies with each day of the menstrual cycle. During menstruation it is shed as far as the basal layer.

Myometrium. The muscle layer (Figure 8.2).

Figure 8.2
Muscle Structure of the Uterus

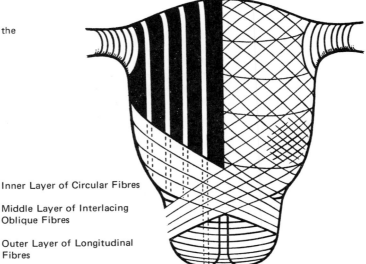

Inner Layer of Circular Fibres

Middle Layer of Interlacing Oblique Fibres

Outer Layer of Longitudinal Fibres

1. Outer layer of longitudinal fibres which pass over the fundus from front to back, starting and finishing at the level of the internal os. Just a few fibres run into the cervix. In labour, as the muscles contract and retract, these help to shorten the upper uterine segment and help to pull up and shorten the cervix.

2. Middle layer of oblique fibres. These pass in both directions and so interlace to form a figure of eight pattern around the blood vessels. They do not extend into the cervix. In the first stage of labour they contract and retract, making the upper uterine segment shorter and thicker and so push the fetus downwards to distend the lower uterine segment. In the second stage of labour their action facilitates expulsion of the fetus. In the

third stage of labour further retraction occurs and as the fibres become still shorter and thicker, pressure is put on the blood vessels which they surround. Following placental separation this action controls post-partum haemorrhage. These fibres are sometimes described as nature's 'living ligatures', and they are certainly arranged plentifully at the sides of the uterus where the uterine arteries flow.

3. Inner layer of circular fibres which are arranged very thickly around the cornua and in the lower uterine segment but very sparsely in the uterine body. It is the weakest of the three layers but an extremely important one as it allows dilatation of the cervix as the fetus descends.

Perimetrium or peritoneum, covers the uterus quite smoothly and almost entirely. The areas which are excluded are (1) those areas of cervix previously mentioned, and (2) a narrow strip of the lateral uterine walls. It is attached quite firmly to the uterus except for an anterior portion of the isthmus where its loose attachment allows the bladder to expand.

Blood Supply

Ovarian arteries on the right and left from the abdominal aorta, supply the fundus of the uterus. They pass downwards to meet the uterine artery of the corresponding side.

Uterine arteries on the right and left reach the uterus at the level of the internal os, and send branches to supply the body of the uterus as well as the cervix and vagina.

Venous drainage is into the ovarian veins which drain into the inferior vena cava on the right side, and into the renal vein on the left.

Lymphatic Drainage

Lymphatic drainage is into the internal iliac and the sacral glands.

Nerve Supply

Sympathetic and parasympathetic nerves from the Lee Frankenhauser plexus.

Supports

The round ligaments: maintain the uterus in its position of anteversion and anteflexion. They extend from the cornua at each side, pass downwards and insert into the tissues of the labia majora.

The broad ligaments: which are not true ligaments but folds of peritoneum extending laterally between the uterus and side walls of the pelvis.

The cardinal ligaments, pubocervical ligaments and *uterosacral ligaments* although described as supporting ligaments of the cervix are obviously also uterine supports. Overstretching of these ligaments will result in prolapse of the uterus.

Functions

1. To prepare a bed for the fertilised ovum.
2. To nourish the fertilised ovum for the gestation period.
3. To expel the products of conception at full term.
4. To involute following childbirth.

Relations

1. *Anterior*: as for the cervix. The intestines lie above the bladder and in front of the body of the uterus.
2. *Posterior*: relations of the cervix and uterosacral ligaments.
3. *Lateral*: relations of the cervix, the fallopian tubes, ovaries, and round ligaments.
4. *Superior*: the intestines.
5. *Inferior*: the vagina.

The diagram showing relations of the vagina (Figure 6.1) also shows relations of the cervix and the body of the uterus.

THE PREGNANT UTERUS

Situation

By the twelfth week of pregnancy, the uterus is rising out of the pelvis to become an abdominal organ. It is no longer anteverted and anteflexed but is becoming vertical. As it rises in the abdomen it leans towards the right. It reaches the umbilicus by the twenty-fourth week and the xiphisternum by the thirty-sixth week. Following the thirty-sixth week, the height of the fundus drops a little, because the fetal head starts to descend into the pelvis.

Shape

As the cavity of the uterus fills with the growing embryo so the uterus becomes globular in shape. Between the twelfth and thirty-sixth week it becomes ovoid as the fetus grows longer and, subsequently, as the fetal head descends into the pelvis it becomes globular again.

Size

The number of weeks of gestation can be estimated by palpating the size of the uterus abdominally. It is known that at full term, i.e. a forty-week gestation period, the uterus measures approximately 30 cm (12 in) in length, 23 cm (9 in) in width and is about 20 cm (8 in) thick. The weight is increased from 57 g to approximately 1 kilogram.

Gross Structure

The cervix in its pregnant state has been described.

The isthmus with the cervix develops to form the lower uterine segment.

The cavity is obviously no longer an empty hollow but is filled with the products of conception.

Microscopic Structure

Endometrium. Once the fertilised ovum has embedded, the uterine lining is re-named the *decidua* and becomes much thicker and more vascular than the non-pregnant endometrium. The glands become more vascular and their secretion is increased. These changes occur as the result of increased hormone activity.

Myometrium. Each muscle fibre increases ten times in length and at least three times in width, as well as there being a considerable amount of new muscle growth. The three layers of muscle become much more clearly defined. Painless contractions of the uterine muscles occur throughout pregnancy from the eighth week onwards. These are known as Braxton Hicks contractions, and although they have no actual function during these early weeks they are nevertheless preparing the uterus for its supreme effort during labour.

Perimetrium. This grows at a corresponding rate with the uterus and continues to lie smoothly over it.

Blood Supply and Lymphatic Drainage

Both the blood and lymphatic vessels enlarge in order to keep pace with the work of the growing uterus.

Supports

The ligaments are composed mainly of smooth muscle and, under the influence of progesterone, thicken and relax to some extent. The greatest strain is put on the round ligaments whose normal function is to keep the uterus anteverted and anteflexed.

THE UTERUS IN LABOUR

First Stage
(Figure 8.3a)

Labour begins with the onset of regular and rhythmical contractions of the uterine muscles. The longitudinal and oblique muscle fibres of the upper segment are capable of retraction as well as of contraction and this action results in shortening and thickening of the upper segment. The fetus is thus pushed downwards causing the circular fibres in the lower segment to dilate. The internal os dilates first, making the cervix funnel shaped.

This opposing action of the two uterine segments, i.e. the upper uterine segment becomes short and thick while the lower uterine segment thins and dilates, is known as the **polarity** of the uterus.

As a result of this continued action a line of demarcation occurs between the two segments. Known as the **retraction ring**, this cannot be seen unless the uterus is exposed as at Caesarean section.

While the muscles of the upper segment are shortening and so pulling upwards, the longitudinal fibres extending into the cervix are pulling up and shortening that structure. As the contractions become stronger and more frequent, the cervix is completely withdrawn into the lower segment and dilates simultaneously as the fetal head is directed downwards.

When the cervix has opened widely enough to allow the fetal head to pass through, it is said to be '**fully dilated**', and this marks the completion of the first stage of labour (*see* Figure 7.2).

Second Stage

The uterine contractions become stronger, longer, and more frequent. Their character changes and they become more expulsive in nature, thus forcing the fetus through the widely opened cervix and right through the birth canal.

Figure 8.3
The Uterus in Labour:
(a) first stage (b) second
stage: separation and
descent of placenta (c)
third stage: expulsion of
placenta. Uterus further
contracts and retracts to
control haemorrhage

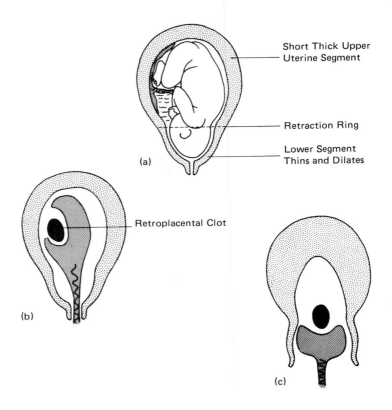

Short Thick Upper Uterine Segment

Retraction Ring

Lower Segment Thins and Dilates

(a)

Retroplacental Clot

(b)

(c)

Third Stage

As the fetal body is expelled, further muscle contraction and re-traction occurs causing the upper uterine segment to diminish in size. The placenta is not made of elastic tissue and is therefore forced off the uterine wall, separation usually commencing in the centre of the placenta, and extending to the circumference. This separation is possible because of the presence of a layer of per-forated cells between the endometrium and myometrium, the layer of Nitabuch (Figure 8.3b).

When the mechanism of placental separation is completed, the placenta is pushed into the lower uterine segment by further con-tractions in the upper segment. The lower segment being dilated results in the upper segment contracting and retracting still further to become even shorter and thicker (polarity of the uterus, Figure 8.3c). In this way the muscle fibres apply pressure to the blood vessels and haemorrhage from the placental site is control-led (Figure 8.4).

It is possible to appreciate this contraction and retraction of the uterus by abdominal palpation when it is recognised by find-ing a firm, hard mass of cricket-ball like consistency.

At the end of the third stage of labour the uterus is approxi-mately 15 cm (6 in) in length, 10 cm (4 in) in width and 7.5 cm (3 in) in depth.

Figure 8.4
'Living Ligature' Action of
Uterine Muscle: (a) relaxed
uterine muscle fibres
surrounding blood vessels
(b) contracted fibres
showing 'living ligature'
action

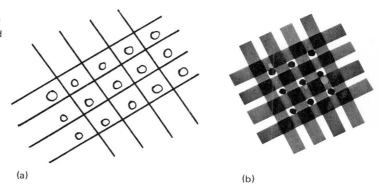

(a)　　　　　　　　　　(b)

THE UTERUS IN THE PUERPERIUM

The puerperium is a period of from six to eight weeks following childbirth, during which time the genital organs return to their pre-pregnant state, lactation should be established, and the new infant accepted into the family. The uterus which developed over a forty-week period during pregnancy has now a much shorter time in which to make regressive changes.

Situation

Immediately following the third stage of labour the fundus of the uterus is found about halfway between the symphysis pubis and the umbilicus. Within the next twenty-four hours the lower uterine segment regains its tone and, consequently, pushes up the fundus to the level of the umbilicus. If the uterus is then palpated on each successive day, it is found to be a finger-breadth lower in the abdomen at each examination. By the tenth day of the puerperium it can no longer be palpated abdominally, because anteversion and anteflexion are almost complete.

Shape

When the placenta has been expelled the uterus contracts and retracts and becomes globular in shape. As involution takes place the cavity becomes smaller, and six weeks following delivery the uterus has returned to its original, pear-like shape.

Size

At the end of labour, the uterus is approximately 15 cm (6 in) long, 10 cm (4 in) wide, 7.5 cm (3 in) thick and weighs 0.9 kg (2 lb). During the first week of puerperium it loses 0.45 kg (1 lb) in weight and a further 0.2 kg (8 oz) in the second week. At the end of the puerperium it is once again 7.5 cm (3 in) long, 5 cm (2 in) wide, 2.5 cm (1 in) thick and weighs 57 g (2 oz).

Gross Structure

The changes in the cervix have already been described, and while these are in progress the isthmus begins to reform and the uterine cavity to close.

Microscopic Structure

Decidua. The lining of the uterus is shed down to the basal layer and a new endometrium begins to form. The vaginal discharge of decidua, blood, and lymph is known as the *lochia*. As the uterus contracts in order to expel blood clots, 'after pains' are often experienced. These pains can be relieved by mild analgesic drugs, and 0.5 mg ergometrine given orally or by intra-muscular injection will produce stronger uterine contractions to expel the clots.

Myometrium. The uterine muscle continues to contract even when labour is completed. This restricts the blood supply to the muscle fibres and, when a certain degree of ischaemia (anaemia) has been reached, certain ferments are produced. These ferments cause autolysis (self digestion) of the muscle fibres and the protoplasm which is broken down is passed into the general circulation, and excreted by the kidneys in the urine. This process is continued until the muscle fibres have returned to their non-pregnant condition.

Perimetrium. This shrinks at the same rate as the uterus and remains as a smooth outer covering.

Blood Supply

Because of the pressure exerted by the retracted uterine muscle fibres, the blood in the uterine vessels clots. Simultaneously with absorption of this clot, new smaller blood vessels develop within the old ones resulting in their re-canalisation and a less abundant blood supply to the now non-pregnant uterus.

Supports

The supporting ligaments of the uterus will regain their tone more quickly if post-natal exercises are taught and supervised during the first ten days of the puerperium (the lying-in period). They should be practised for a few minutes several times a day until the six-week period of the puerperium has been completed.

Post-natal Examination

The post-natal examination has been previously mentioned but the necessity of examining the uterus and cervix can well be stressed once again.

1. The cervix should be examined with a light and a speculum to ensure that it is healthy. A smear for cervical cytology should be made wherever this is possible.

2. Palpation of the uterus to ensure that it is anteverted, anteflexed, and of correct size. Prolapse and retroversion of the uterus causes backache and pelvic discomfort and both conditions require treatment.

3. Red lochia may indicate retained products if involution of the uterus is not complete. Secondary post-partum haemorrhage is likely to occur if this condition is not treated.

It is our duty as midwives, therefore, that we should not feel our 'labours' are complete until each patient that we have delivered has also been seen by her general practitioner or by a consultant for this post-natal check. We can then be satisfied that neither the patient's general health, nor her genital organs have been adversely affected by childbearing.

SPECIMEN
QUESTIONS

Describe the shape, size, and structure of the uterus at term. What changes does it undergo during each stage of labour?

Describe the structure of the uterus, the changes which take place in it during pregnancy, and the way in which the uterus prevents haemorrhage after the birth of the baby.

Describe the supports of the uterus. How may they be damaged in labour? How can the risk of such damage be reduced?

Describe the uterine muscle and its action in all the stages of labour.

Describe the anatomy of the body of the uterus. Describe the muscle action of the uterus in the third stage of labour.

What changes take place in the uterus during the puerperium? What may interfere with normal involution?

Outline the anatomy of the body of the uterus. Describe the behaviour of its musculature in the three stages of labour.

9
The Fallopian Tubes and Ovaries

THE FALLOPIAN TUBES

Situation

Each tube extends from the cornu of the uterus, travels towards the side walls of the pelvis, then turns downwards and backwards before reaching it. The tubes lie within the broad ligament.

Shape

They are tubes. The lumen of each communicates with the cavity of the uterus superiorly, and the peritoneal cavity inferiorly.

Size

The length of each tube is approximately 10 cm (4 in) and the diameter about 3 mm (0.12 in).

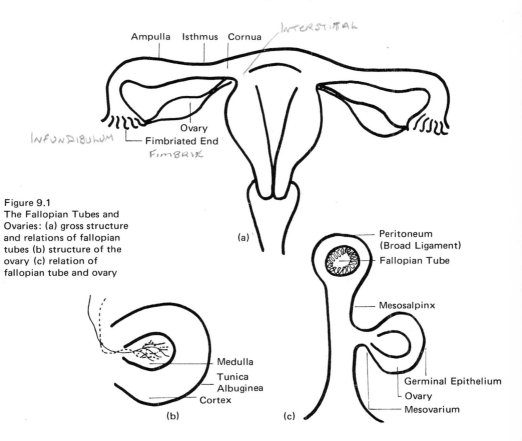

Figure 9.1
The Fallopian Tubes and Ovaries: (a) gross structure and relations of fallopian tubes (b) structure of the ovary (c) relation of fallopian tube and ovary

Gross Structure
(Figure 9.1)

The *Interstitial portion* lies within the wall of the uterus. The narrowest part of the tube is the *isthmus.*

The *ampulla* is the widened out area where fertilisation is thought to occur.

The *infundibulum,* or fimbriated end, is the terminal portion which turns backwards and downwards, and ends in finger-like processes which surround the orifice of the tube.

Microscopic Structure

Ciliated epithelium forms the lining of the tube and aids the passage of the ovum to the uterus. This epithelium is arranged in folds (plicae) which slow down the journey of the fertilised ovum, thus giving it time to develop and so be ready for embedding when it reaches the uterus.

Connective tissue lies beneath the epithelium.

Muscle coat is arranged in two layers:
1. inner layer of circular fibres
2. outer layer of longitudinal fibres

Peritoneum hangs over the tubes but is absent on their inferior surface.

Blood Supply

The blood supply comes from the uterine and ovarian arteries; venous return is by corresponding veins.

Lymphatic Drainage

The lymphatic drainage is into the lumbar glands.

Nerve Supply

The nerve supply is from the ovarian plexus.

Supports

The infundibulo-pelvic ligaments. These are formed from folds of the broad ligament and run from the infundibulum of the tube to the side walls of the pelvis.

Function

The tube forms a canal through which the ovum and sperm can pass, unite, and commence early development.

Relations

1. *Anterior:*
2. *Posterior:* } the peritoneal cavity and the intestines.
3. *Superior:*
4. *Inferior*: the broad ligament and the ovaries.
5. *Lateral*: infundibulo-pelvic ligaments and side walls of the pelvis.
6. *Medial*: the uterus.

Obstetric Conditions Associated with the Fallopian Tubes
Infertility

Investigations among women at infertility clinics show that in about 30 per cent of patients, pregnancy has been prevented by an obstructed fallopian tube. This partial or complete obstruction is often the result of previous tubal or generalised pelvic infection.

Insufflation is carried out to test tubal patency and, in some cases, the insufflation actually removes the obstruction: many women conceive after the investigation has been performed.

Ectopic Gestation

An ectopic gestation is a pregnancy which develops outside the uterus. This most commonly occurs in the fallopian tube. The causes of a tubal pregnancy have not really been determined, but an obstructed tube will obviously be a predisposing factor. There is also said to be a higher incidence in those women who use an intra-uterine contraceptive device. If the embryo develops in the isthmus, the narrowest part of the tube, it soon erodes through the thin layer of tissues in the embedding process, ruptures the tube, and opens up large blood vessels, causing an intraperitoneal haemorrhage. The condition is then known as a **ruptured ectopic gestation,** and constitutes an acute abdominal catastrophe. Blood transfusion, followed by prompt surgical operation in which the tube is excised, become essentially life-saving operations.

Sterilisation

When further pregnancies are likely to endanger a mother's health and well-being, some obstetricians offer their patients the operation for sterilisation and most patients gladly accept this offer. The operation entails the clamping and cutting of each fallopian tube. Each cut end is then ligated and buried. More recent treatment involves laparoscopy and treating the fallopian tubes by a diathermy needle to seal them. There is then no opportunity for the ovum and sperm to meet and fertilisation cannot occur.

Fallopian tubes — Ovaries become an abdominal organ elongate idue to pt rech. to progesterone.

THE OVARIES

Situation

The two ovaries lie within the peritoneal cavity in a small depression of the posterior wall of the broad ligament. They are situated at the fimbriated end of the fallopian tube, at about the level of the pelvic brim.

Shape

Small almond-like organs, dull white in colour and with a corrugated surface.

Size

3 cm x 2 cm x 1 cm.

Gross Structure

This varies with the age of the woman:

Birth to Puberty

The organs are smooth, dull white, and rather solid in consistency.

Menstrual Phase

Between puberty and the menopause the organs are larger and are rather irregular on the surface, more like a walnut than an almond.

Post-menopausal Phase

The ovaries become smaller and shrunken, and are covered with scar tissue where, month after month, the graafian follicles have ruptured.

Microscopic Structure

Germinal epithelium is another name for the peritoneum which encloses the ovary.

Tunica albuginea, the tough, fibrous, outer coat.

Cortex consists mostly of stroma in which graafian follicles are embedded. These follicles each contain an ovum and can be found at varying degrees of development. The **corpus luteum** is the scar tissue which forms after a follicle has burst. The cortex is, therefore, the 'working' part of the ovary.

Medulla is the central portion and point of entry for blood vessels, lymphatics, and nerves. It consists chiefly of fibrous and elastic tissue.

Blood Supply

The blood is supplied from the ovarian arteries; venous drainage into the ovarian veins.

Lymphatic Drainage

Lymphatic drainage is into the lumbar glands.

Nerve Supply

The nerve supply is from the ovarian plexus.

Supports

The fossa in which the ovary lies. Where it is attached to the broad ligament is called the **mesovarium**. The broad ligament which extends between the fallopian tubes and the ovary is known as the **mesosalpinx**.

Function

To produce ova for fertilisation, oestrogen and progesterone.

Relations

1. *Anterior*: the broad ligament.
2. *Lateral*: the fallopian tube.

Ovulation
Graafian Follicle

In the cortex of each ovary of every female child nearly 200,000 primordial follicles can be found. As the child grows, these primitive structures become more mature and are known then as **graafian follicles**. With the onset of puberty one follicle develops more rapidly each month than the others. It fills with fluid, rises to the surface of the ovary and then, bursting through it, ruptures, to release the fluid and the ovum it contains.

Corpus Luteum

The remaining shell of the graafian follicle is known as the **corpus luteum**. If the ovum is not fertilised, fibrosis occurs and the structure is then called the **corpus albicans** and, in the final stages of fibrosis, it is called the **corpus fibrosum**. It is these scars on the surface of the ovary which give it its shrivelled, post-menopausal appearance.

Normally, ovulation occurs only once in each month, and it is an accepted fact that each ovary, every alternate month, releases one ovum. Should the ovum become fertilised, then the corpus luteum does not shrivel but increases in size. It produces sufficient gonadotropic hormone to maintain the pregnancy until the placenta has developed sufficiently to fulfil its own function.

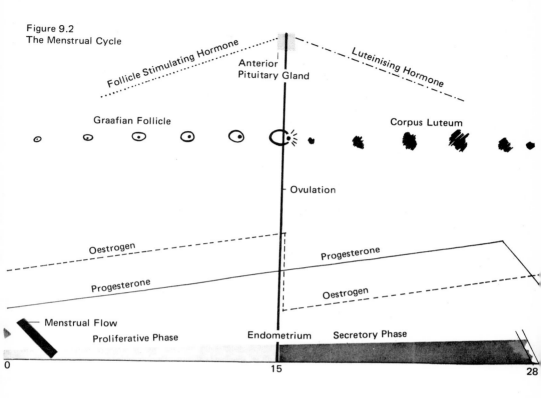

Figure 9.2
The Menstrual Cycle

The Menstrual Cycle
(Figure 9.2)

The length of the average menstrual cycle covers a period of twenty-eight days and this is divided into four phases:

Regenerative Phase

During the first few days of this phase, the endometrium of the uterus is shed right down to the basal layer.

The anterior pituitary gland releases the **follicle stimulating hormone** causing the **graafian follicle** to increase in size. This results in a rising level of circulating oestrogen, and this alteration in the balance of hormones causes new growth of the endometrium.

If the length of the menstrual cycle is more or less than twenty-eight days, it is this regenerative phase that is variable.

Ovulation

There comes a time when the graafian follicle has increased to such an extent that it must rupture. With its rupture, the ovum is released and the oestrogen level drops.

Secretory Phase

The ruptured follicle, now known as the **corpus luteum** is stimulated by the luteinising hormone from the anterior pituitary gland. (The follicle stimulating hormone being simultaneously withdrawn). The corpus luteum now begins to increase in size and to produce progesterone in increasing amounts. This further change in hormone balance stimulates the uterus to prepare its lining for the reception of a fertilised ovum and it undergoes the following secretory changes:

1. The endometrium becomes much thicker and more spongy.
2. The blood supply is increased.
3. There is increased activity of the secretory glands.
4. Mineral salts and glucose are deposited.

Menstruation

If the ovum is not fertilised, the anterior pituitary withdraws the luteinising hormone after fourteen to fifteen days. Preparations for pregnancy cease and the endometrium is shed with the menstrual flow. As the luteinising hormone is withdrawn, the anterior pituitary gland once again prepares for pregnancy by releasing the follicle stimulating hormone and another regenerative phase begins.

The Cyclical Syndrome

The changes in hormone balance which occur during the menstrual cycle inevitably cause changes throughout the body. To some extent, the early signs and symptoms of pregnancy are experienced during the second half of the cycle, but to the majority of women these are only transitory discomforts accepted as being inevitable and medical advice is rarely sought, or, indeed, needed. The most common symptoms experienced are:

1. Enlargement and tenderness of breasts and nipples.
2. Fluid in the breast.
3. Digestive disturbances, e.g. epigastric discomfort, heartburn and constipation.
4. Increased frequency of micturition.
5. Increased amount of vaginal discharge.
6. Increased activity of the skin.
7. Weight gain.

These conditions are largely brought about by the relaxation of smooth muscle caused by progesterone. Proliferation of tissues in the breast and genital tract, resulting from hormonal influence, accounts for the symptoms experienced directly there. Retention of mineral salts leads to retention of body fluid causing oedema and weight gain. This is probably also the causative factor of headaches and visual disturbances. Some women actually become sleepy and inert probably due to deposits of glucose in the uterine lining.

During the secretory phase it has become an established fact that judgement is impaired. Careless mistakes are made, women are more accident prone, and the behaviour of schoolgirls is said to worsen.

The majority of women accept all these things as inevitable — they probably do not even think about them — and are certainly not incapacitated by them. A minority present with more severe symptoms which they cannot control. Due to less well balanced endocrine activity they complain of nervous tension, irritability, depression, and are generally difficult to live with. These women should be advised to seek medical advice if their symptoms do not abate; treatment lies in a combination of reassurance, controlled diet, and drugs. Low salt intake and diuretics are used to combat fluid retention and oedema; adequate roughage in the diet and aperients to treat constipation. Tranquillising drugs reduce the degree of irritability and depression is counteracted with drugs of the stimulant group.

It is also worth remembering that conditions such as asthma, migraine, and epilepsy are sometimes exacerbated in the secretory phase of the menstrual cycle and, if this is so, a similar exacerbation should be watched for during pregnancy.

Conception and Contraception
Conception

The optimum time for a pregnancy to be initiated is within twenty-four hours of ovulation. Intercourse during the twenty-four hours preceding ovulation will supply sperms to the fallopian tubes, waiting expectantly for the appearance of the ovum. It is, therefore, important to each woman trying to conceive, that she know the approximate date of ovulation. Records should be kept over a period of months charting the first day of each menstrual period and, thus, calculating the time of ovulation as being fifteen days prior to that particular period. In this way, the days of successive months when she is likely to start menstruating, and therefore the days when she is likely to ovulate, can be estimated.

If the menses are irregular, such calculation is impossible. However, it has been realised that the body temperature is raised by 0.5°C at the time of ovulation. For some women, therefore, a daily recording of the oral temperature, taken immediately upon waking in the early morning, is a more accurate method of estimating their time of ovulation.

Contraception—the 'Safe' Period

This is a very misleading term. The name is wrongfully applied because the method is certainly not a reliable way of avoiding pregnancy. It is only considered when the chemical or mechanical devices required are either unacceptable or unobtainable.

The life span of the ovum is not actually known, but the sperms once inside the uterus probably survive for about five days. When considering contraception it is therefore advisable to leave a wide margin when intercourse must be avoided on each side of the expected date of ovulation. Therefore, presuming that the menstrual cycle is an average one of twenty-eight days, intercourse should be avoided between the tenth and twentieth days inclusively.

—Coitus Interruptus

Like the safe period, this method is only considered when the usual contraceptive devices are not acceptable. Neither partner is able to achieve complete sexual satisfaction and the technique can only result in physical and mental tension. Harmonious relationships cannot be maintained by this method, or by complete abstinence from intercourse, and both methods should be considered harmful.

—Mechanical Devices

A rubber sheath can be worn by the male to prevent seminal fluid from entering the vagina, but it sometimes has disadvantages. Many men find it bothersome to use, to others it causes irritation and lack of potency, while many partners complain that it reduces the pleasure of intimate contact. It is one of the more reliable methods of contraception, although there is always the possibility that the sheath may rupture or become dislodged during intercourse. For this reason the female partner should use one of the chemical preparations when her partner uses a sheath.

The female can be fitted with a rubber cap which fits completely over the cervix and so occludes the entrance to the uterus. The cap comes in a variety of designs and sizes and should be fitted by a person fully trained in family planning techniques. It should be used with a chemical preparation and not removed until at least eight hours following intercourse.

In recent years, intra-uterine contraceptives made of pliable plastic material have been available. These devices do not interfere with normal uterine action nor do they prevent union of the ovum and sperm. Their contraceptive action is still not understood, but they are thought to have a local effect on the uterine endometrium and so prevent implantation of a fertilised ovum.

The disadvantage of this particular method lies in the fact that the device may be unknowingly expelled by the wearer and that pregnancy may occur through no faulty technique of her own. Also, as has been previously mentioned, there is an increased risk of ectopic pregnancy. Some women find the intra-uterine device unacceptable because for them it produces excessive menstrual bleeding and uterine cramps.

—the 'Pill'

The surest way of preventing pregnancy is for the female partner to take the contraceptive pill. There are several types of this pill but they each contain carefully balanced oestrogen/progesterone hormones which inhibit ovulation. The pill is prescribed only under strict medical supervision and is controlled by Schedule 4 of the Drugs Act. To be fully effective the pills must be taken exactly as the instructions state.

Some women suffer from mild but unpleasant side effects, and this method is not acceptable to them.

Describe the pathway through which the fertilised egg passes in order to reach the uterus. What may happen if anything obstructs the passage of the fertilised egg into the uterus?

Describe the structure of the ovary. What hormones does it produce and what influence do they have on the course of pregnancy?

Describe the anatomy and physiology of the ovaries.

What is a hormone? Describe the menstrual cycle paying particular attention to the controlling role of hormones in its regulation.

At which time. in the menstrual cycle is pregnancy (*a*) most likely to occur, (*b*) least likely to occur? Show how pregnancy may be prevented by the administration of a hormone.

Draw a diagram to show the relationship during the menstrual cycle between ovulation, the thickness of the endometrium and the concentration of oestrogen and progesterone in the blood stream.

Discuss the advantages and disadvantages of three different contraceptives.

10

The Male Reproductive System

Like the female reproductive system, the male has both internal and external organs of reproduction.

Situation

Externally lies the penis which transmits the **urethra,** and the **scrotum** which contains the **testes, epididymides** and part of the **vas deferens.** Internally lie the **vas deferens—seminal vesicles and ducts—ejaculatory ducts—prostate gland—bulbo-urethral (or Cowpers) glands.**

The Penis

This is suspended between the thighs, hanging downwards in front of the scrotal sac. It is expanded at the distal end to form an acorn-shaped structure, the **glans penis.** The penis is composed of three columns of sponge-like erectile tissue with a rich blood supply. This is enclosed in a firm sheath of fibrous tissue and is covered with skin which is continuous with that of the scrotum and groins. The skin covering the glans penis is doubled back on itself to form the **prepuce** or **foreskin.** It is this fold of skin which is removed during the operation of **circumcision.**

The penis transmits a portion of the urethra which acts as a passage for semen as well as for excretion of urine. A small

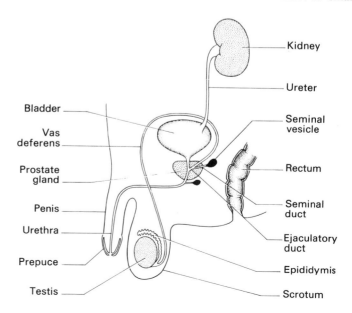

Figure 10.1
The Male Organs of
Reproduction

sphincter prevents semen from entering the bladder and the simultaneous passage of sperm and urine.

Sexual arousal results in the usually limp hanging penis becoming larger, rounder and firmer and causing it to stand erect as stimulation of the nervous system increases the blood supply to the organ.

Boys should be told before the onset of puberty that such erections are likely to occur as the result of excitement, sexual or otherwise. They should also be told that when they begin to produce sperms, 'wet dreams' (**nocturnal emissions**) are liable to occur as the result of erotic dreams. It should be emphasised that this is quite normal since adolescent boys show the same concern about their reproductive functions as girls show about menstruation.

The Scrotum

This is a pouch-like sac, covered with skin, from which the penis hangs. It is divided by a fibrous septum into two cavities each of which contains a **testis epididymus** and the initial portion of the vas deferens.

The Testes (or Testicles)

The male reproductive glands. They are formed in the foetal abdomen about the twenty-eighth week of intra-uterine life and descend into the scrotum to be supported by the spermatic cord, before birth. The testes do not function fully until stimulated by the anterior pituitary gland at puberty.

Size, Shape & Appearance

In appearance the testes are oval structures, white in colour, about 4 cm long, 2.5 cm wide and 3 cm thick, weighing 10—14 g.

Structure

Their glandular tissue is divided into 200—300 lobes. Each lobe contains convoluted **seminiferous tubules** lined with germinal epithelium from which the sperm are produced after puberty.

Between the tubules are interstitial cells which produce testosterone.

Functions

The testes have two functions:

1. To produce testosterone, the hormone which controls secondary male sex characteristics.
2. To produce spermatozoa.

The function of the testes can be affected by **orchitis** which can result from mumps or other acute infections. Such an infection can result in failure of the testes to produce spermatozoa.

Epididymides

These are fine convoluted tubules about 6 metres in length which connect the testes and the vas deferens. The sperm are stored here to become mature and motile.

Vas Deferens

Tubes which connect the epididymides to the seminal ducts. These are the tubes which are ligated or cut during the operation of **vasectomy**. Although sperm are still produced they cannot be ejaculated because their passage is obstructed.

Seminal Vesicles

Small irregular shaped sacs about 5 cm long lying between the base of the bladder and the rectum. Their function is to secrete a thick yellowish coloured fluid which is added to the sperm to form seminal fluid. It contains glucose and other substances to nourish the sperm. Each vesicle opens into a **seminal duct** which joins the vas deferens on the corresponding side to form the **ejaculatory duct**.

Ejaculatory Ducts

Each duct is formed by the union of the vas deferens and the seminal duct. The ejaculatory ducts are approximately 2.5 cm long. They pass through the **prostate gland** and join the urethra. So in effect, they connect the vas deferens and urethra.

Prostate Gland

A cone shaped structure 4 cm long, 3 cm wide, 2 cm deep, weighing about 8 g. It surrounds the upper part of the urethra and lies in direct contact with the neck of the bladder. It is composed of glandular tissue and involuntary muscle fibres and is enclosed in a fibrous capsule. Secretions of the prostate gland are added to the sperm and seminal fluid as they pass into the urethra. The muscle tissue of the gland aids in ejaculation of the sperm. The prostate gland quite commonly becomes enlarged in elderly men and if pressure on the urethral sphincter or the urethra itself occurs, then acute retention of urine results. The condition can be relieved by passing a catheter into the bladder or by prostatectomy in suitable patients.

Bulbo-Urethral (Cowpers) Glands

Small glands about the size of a pea, yellow in colour, lying just below the prostate gland. Their ducts, about 3 cm long, open into the urethra before it reaches the penile portion. Secretions from the glands are added to the **seminal fluid** and also help to lubricate the penis during sexual activity.

Seminal Fluid

The fluid in which the spermatozoa are suspended. It nourishes them and aids their motility. Passing from the seminal vesicles and ducts, it travels through the ejaculatory ducts to the urethra where prostatic secretions and secretions from the bulbo-urethral glands are added. It is finally ejaculated during sexual excitement.

PRODUCTION AND PASSAGE OF SPERMATOZOA

Production

As has already been explained, the sperm are produced by the testes, after puberty, from the germinal epithelium of the seminiferous tubules.

Each sperm is a minute cell, having a head which contains the nucleus, a neck, and a tail-like projection which develops a lashing movement and enables the cell to move.

When first produced, the sperm, like other human body cells, contains a nucleus with 46 chromosomes. Before fertilisation of the female cell can occur it is therefore obvious that the chromosome content of both male and female gamete must be reduced to 23. When fertilisation of the ovum by the sperm occurs, the chromosome number is thus restored to 46.

The method of reducing chromosomes is known as **meiosis.**

Meiosis

The 46 chromosomes of the parent cell first arrange themselves in their 23 pairs, each maternal chromosome with its paternal partner. A complicated process of interchange then occurs with the pairs not only intermingling but even parts of individual chromosomes interchanging. The pairs then separate completely with one partner from each pair going to opposite ends of the cell. There are therefore now two nuclei at opposite ends of the cell each containing an assortment of 23 chromosomes.

This meiotic division is then followed by **mitosis** — the usual method of cell reproduction.

Mitosis

The method by which all body cells reproduce in order for growth and repair of tissues to occur. Each body cell has a nucleus of 46 chromosomes. In this type of cell division every chromosome divides into two threads. There are thus two sets of identical chromosomes in the one cell. The cytoplasm then divides giving two cells each containing twenty-three paired chromosomes. Therefore, following meiotic division of the nucleus of the gametes and then further mitosis, the one nucleus containing 46 chromosomes gives rise to four nuclei each containing 23 chromosomes.

In the sperm, these changes are thought to occur in the epididymis. It is here also that the tail of the sperm develops its lashing ability and so enables the sperm to move.

Passage

Once the sperm are motile they are able to travel through the epididymes to the vas deferens. The seminal vesicles pass their secretions through their ducts to be added to the sperm and the prostatic secretions are added through the ejaculatory ducts. The sperm are then passed through the urethral orifice with the semen during sexual activity.

Draw a large fully labelled diagram to illustrate and explain the organs of the male reproductive system.

Write a detailed account of the production, storage and passage of spermatozoa.

Describe the structure and functions of the testes. What conditions might result in male sterility?

Make an illustrated comparison between the surgical procedures of male and female sterilisation.

Describe the following conditions:

1. Cryptorchism
2. Orchitis
3. Hypospadias
4. Phimosis
5. Vasectomy

For what reasons might the operation of circumcision be carried out? What structures are involved?

11

Fertilisation and Development of the Ovum

Fertilisation

Millions of spermatozoa, tadpole-like structures, are deposited by the male in the vagina during sexual intercourse. Each sperm carries 23 chromosomes in its nucleus, as meiosis has taken place. The acidity of the vaginal fluid destroys many sperm but the survivors make their way up through the cervix into the body of the uterus and thence to the fallopian tubes, where the ovum is awaiting fertilisation in one of them.

The sperms that surround the ovum produce hyaluronidase, an enzyme which breaks down the protective protoplasm of the ovum in order to make penetration of the cell a little easier. The head of one sperm then penetrates the ovum, after which its body and tail drop off.

Twenty-three chromosomes in the nucleus of the sperm now pair up with the twenty-three chromosomes in the nucleus of the ovum, so restoring the human cell pattern of chromosomes to 46, arranged in 23 pairs. This pattern is repeated in all cells of the human body regardless of the type of tissue.

Chromosomes

Consist of genetic material commonly called DNA (deoxyribonucleic acid) and protein materials. Because each individual chromosome carries the hereditary material the appearance and characteristics of the new child are determined at the moment of conception and are conveyed from both parents.

Sex determination. One pair of chromosomes are sex-determining, those of the female being designated XX and those of the male XY. The sex of the new child (as well as his appearance and character) will therefore also be determined at the moment of conception. The sex will be dependent upon the way in which the chromosomes split during meiosis and then combine again at fertilisation. For instance, X from the female gamete pairing with X from the sperm will result in XX — a female child; while X from the female gamete pairing with Y from the sperm will result in XY — a male child. As the male carries the Y chromosome it can be seen that it is the male partner who determines the sex of the children.

Inherited Disease

Unfortunately it is not only sex, appearance and personality traits that are carried in the genes, but also medical conditions such as phenylketonuria, which may affect children of either sex.

When sex-linked diseases such as haemophilia are likely to occur, amniocentesis can be performed to determine the sex of the child. The mother may then be offered the choice of having the pregnancy terminated.

Chromosome Abnormalities

Occasionally abnormalities occur in the pairing of chromosomes. Perhaps the best known example of this condition is mongolism, or Down's Syndrome, where there is a trisomy instead of pair 21.

Research in male prisons has shown that many criminals of aggressive nature have an extra Y chromosome — i.e. XYY instead of XY.

Radiation hazards can cause mutation of chromosomes and genes, but sterility or abortion of an abnormal fetus are both more likely than the birth of an infant with congenital abnormalities.

EARLY DEVELOPMENT OF THE PLACENTA

The Zygote
(Figure 11.1a)

The name given to the fertilised ovum is the zygote.

The Morula
(Figure 11.1c)

This is the name given to the round mass of cells which is formed by the division and subdivision of cells as the zygote develops. This method of cell division is known as **mitosis.**

The Blastocyst
(Figure 11.1d)

This is the morula in its next stage of development. Now approximately 2 mm in diameter, some cells in the centre have begun to disintegrate leaving a small space.

The inner cell mass are the cells which remain in the centre of the structure. These will eventually develop to form the fetus and the amniotic sac in which he is contained.

The trophoblast is the outer layer of cells, and from this layer, small root-like structures, **the primitive chorionic villi,** start to grow (Figure 11.1f). Some of these structures will develop to form the placenta and the remainder atrophy to form the chorionic membrane which surrounds the amniotic sac and lines the uterus (Figure 11.1g). This stage of development is reached seven to ten days following conception, during which time the structure is travelling along the fallopian tube, towards the uterus where the endometrium is being prepared for its reception.

Decidua

Following fertilisation of the ovum the endometrium undergoes a continuation of the changes which occur in the secretory phase of the menstrual cycle and it is from then onwards known as the decidua.

Decidua Basalis

The decidua which lies below the area where the ovum beds down is called the decidua basalis.

Figure 11.1
Early Stages of Placental
Development: (a) the
zygote (b) cell division
(c) the morula (d) the
blastocyst (e) blastocyst
with primitive chorionic
villi (f) blastocyst ready to
embed (g) primitive
placenta and chorion (h)
detailed structure of
primitive chorionic villi

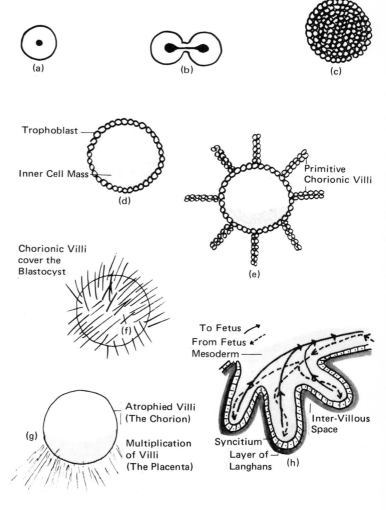

Trophoblast

Inner Cell Mass

(d)

Primitive
Chorionic Villi

(e)

Chorionic Villi
cover the
Blastocyst

(f)

To Fetus
From Fetus
Mesoderm

Atrophied Villi
(The Chorion)

(g)

Multiplication
of Villi
(The Placenta)

Inter-Villous
Space

Syncitium
Layer of
Langhans   (h)

Decidua Capsularis

The decidua capsularis is the area of decidua which encloses the
embedding ovum.

Decidua Vera

The remainder of the uterine lining is called the decidua vera.

    The main function of the chorionic villi is to burrow into the
decidua and cause erosion of maternal tissues and blood vessels.
As the vessels are ruptured so the villi are bathed in pools of
maternal blood, and nourishment is transmitted from the mother's
circulation through the permeable membrane of the villi. At first,
all the villi develop equally but as the embryo increases in size,
the decidua capsularis is pushed further and further outwards and
becomes much thinner. The blood supply in that area is therefore

greatly decreased and the villi atrophy to leave a smooth membrane, the **chorion**, which lines the decidua vera and surrounds the embryonic sac.

In the decidua basalis where a rich blood supply is maintained, the villi multiply rapidly. Some of them bed deeply in the decidua to stabilise the developing placenta while the others branch outwards allowing maternal blood to circulate freely in the intervillous spaces to provide nourishment for further growth of the placenta and fetus. By the fourteenth week of pregnancy the structure of the placenta is fully developed and it occupies about one third of the size of the uterine wall, and the decidua capsularis has been pushed outwards until it lines the cavity of the uterus and lies adjacent to the decidua vera.

Chorionic Gonadtrophin

As the chorionic villi embed in the uterine wall, a hormone called chorionic gonadtrophin is produced. Its function is to stimulate growth and hormone secretion of the corpus luteum and so maintain the pregnancy until the placenta is fully functioning. Chorionic gonadtrophin is secreted in increasing amounts until the end of the first trimester of pregnancy, after which it declines. Because it is produced only by the trophoblast and is excreted in the urine, its presence on urinalysis is a positive indication of pregnancy and this fact is used as the basis for immunological pregnancy diagnosis tests.

Further development of the chorionic villi takes place throughout pregnancy until at full maturity the placenta is about 23 cm (9 in) in diameter, a round flat organ about 2 cm (¾ in) thick in the centre but thinner around the circumference.

Structure of Chorionic Villi (Figure 11.1b)

Each villus is made up as follows:

1. *Syncitium*: a protective layer of protoplasm which surrounds the tiny root-like structure and lines the space between the villi.
2. *Layer of Langhans*: a layer of single cells, the trophoblastic layer.
3. *Mesoderm*: contained within the villus and from which, eventually, the fetal circulatory system develops.

These three layers form a permeable membrane through which the exchange of vital substances from the maternal and fetal circulations takes place. Normally, the blood of the mother and the blood of the fetus never come into direct contact.

DEVELOPMENT OF THE FETUS, UMBILICAL CORD AND AMNIOTIC FLUID

The development of the fetus from the inner cell mass occurs simultaneously with the growth of the placenta from the trophoblast.

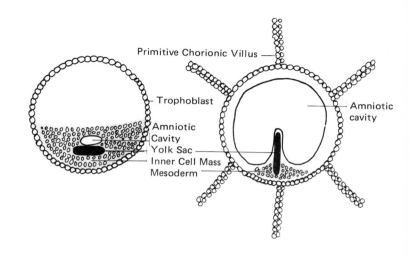

Figure 11.2
Early Development of
Fetus

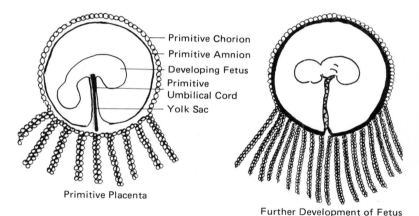

Primitive Placenta

Further Development of Fetus

**Early Development
of Fetus**
(Figure 11.2)

Within the inner cell mass, the first stage in fetal development is the formation of two enclosed cavities which lie adjacent to each other, the amniotic sac and the yolk sac.

The *amniotic sac* is lined with ectoderm, a single layer of cells which is responsible for the growth of fetal skin, hair, nails, teeth, nerve tissue, including that of the sense organs, salivary glands, nasal cavity, and lower part of the anal canal.

The *yolk sac* has a lining of endoderm which develops to form the digestive tract, liver, pancreas, larynx, trachea, lungs, bladder, and the urethra.

Embryonic Plate

Because the amniotic and yolk sacs are adjacent, some ectoderm of the amniotic cavity lies in contact with some of the endoderm of the yolk sac. This area is known as the embryonic plate and is the site of fetal development.

Mesoderm

This is the remainder of the tissue of the inner cell mass. Some of it lies around the embryonic plate. The further development of mesoderm produces the circulatory and lymphatic systems, the skeleton, muscles, kidneys, ureters, and sex organs.

By an action similar to that of the single celled amoeba ingesting food, the amniotic cavity alters its shape in order to surround the yolk sac and mesoderm and draws these tissues into itself.

Umbilical Cord

A duct forms between the amniotic sac and the yolk sac and develops to become the umbilical cord. Two arteries and one vein form from the mesoderm and these blood vessels are a continuation of the smaller vessels which form from the mesoderm within the primitive chorionic villi. Important chemical substances are thus transmitted between the placenta and the fetus. The umbilical vessels are surrounded and protected by a jelly-like substance, and the cord is covered with amnion which is continuous with the skin of the fetus. At full term the cord is 40—50 cm long and is about as thick as a man's thumb.

It is important that the midwife should check the umbilical cord vessels when carrying out placental examination following the third stage of labour. Occasionally a primitive structure remains revealing four blood vessels in the cord, or only two vessels appear to be present. If such an abnormality is present the cord should be sent to the laboratory for investigation since fetal abnormalities are likely, and the newborn infant should be carefully examined and observed. Some such abnormalities are incompatible with life and the fetus may be aborted.

Amniotic Membrane

As the developing fetus enlarges so the amniotic cavity is pushed further and further outwards until the cavity of the uterus is filled. (Simultaneously, as already stated, this is when the decidua capsularis is pushed outwards to lie against the decidua vera and the chorionic membrane is formed as the villi atrophy.) At this stage, therefore, the uterus is lined with chorion, and the amnion forming the fetal sac lies within the chorionic membrane and covers the cord, or body stalk, which connects the fetus with the developing placenta.

Amniotic Fluid

The increasing size of the amniotic cavity is due partly to the developing fetus and partly to the presence of fluid which appears soon after the cavity is formed. The fluid is thought to be secreted by the amniotic membrane and is a clear, straw coloured fluid, alkaline in reaction. During pregnancy it allows free movement of the fetus, protects him from injury, equalises the intra-uterine pressure and helps to maintain a consistent intra-uterine temperature. At the onset of labour there is an average of one litre of amniotic fluid in the uterus which equalises pressure on the fetus during labour contractions. Providing that the sac of fluid remains intact until labour is well advanced, it acts as a cushion to protect the fetal head from pressure as well as acting as a wedge to aid dilatation of the cervix. Immediately prior to delivery when the amniotic sac is ruptured the birth canal is provided with a sterile douche.

Abnormalities of Amniotic Fluid

1. *Polyhydramnios.* An excessive amount of amniotic fluid which tends to be associated with maternal diabetes, abnormalities of the fetal nervous system, oesophageal atresia and uniovular twins. Malpresentation of the fetus is common and prolapse of the cord is more likely to occur.

2. *Oligohydramnios.* A diminished amount of amniotic fluid which does not allow adequate fetal movements. In some instances there is not enough fluid to allow adequate fetal movement and the infant when born may need physiotherapy treatment. His skin is often leathery in appearance. Oligohydramnios is also associated with the very rare condition of renal agenesis.

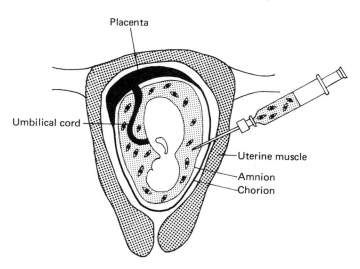

Placenta

Umbilical cord

Uterine muscle

Amnion

Chorion

Figure 11.3
Amniocentesis

Amniocentesis
(Figure 11.3)

A method of obtaining amniotic fluid by introducing a fine trocar and cannula into the amniotic cavity through the abdominal and uterine wall. A local anaesthetic is used. Fetal cells are shed into the amniotic fluid and can be examined to show the sex of the fetus and so the probability of sex linked disease, chromosome abnormalities such as those found in Down's Syndrome and some metabolic diseases. If alpha-fetoprotein is discovered then spina bifida or anencephaly can be diagnosed. If any of these conditions are suspected then amniocentesis is carried out in the middle of pregnancy so that the mother can be offered termination of pregnancy. Later in pregnancy, amniocentesis may be performed to establish the degree of haemolytic disease of the fetus when Rhesus incompatibility is present. Fortunately, this is now a preventable condition so the procedure is less common for this reason. Occasionally, when a mother has an excessive amount of amniotic fluid, amniocentesis may be performed to keep her more comfortable. Other more rare occasions include the assessing of fetal lung maturity when induction of labour is being considered, and to administer an intraperitoneal blood transfusion to the fetus.

Later Fetal Development

Four weeks: following conception, the head of the fetus can be distinguished with rudimentary eyes and ears.

Six weeks: the heart is formed and beating, limb buds are beginning to develop.

Eight weeks: fingers and toes are present on the hands and feet. The external genitalia are beginning to develop.

Twelve weeks: the head is a normal shape, although large in comparison with the body.

Table 11.1 The Monthly Growth of Fetus

	Length		*Weight*	
8 weeks	4 cm	(1.5 in)	negligible	
12 weeks	7.5 cm	(3 in)	14 g	(0.5 oz)
16 weeks	15 cm	(6 in)	113 g	(4 oz)
20 weeks	25 cm	(10 in)	227 g	(8 oz)
24 weeks	30 cm	(12 in)	0.7 kg	(1.5 lb)
28 weeks	35.5 cm	(14 in)	1.2 kg	(2.5 lb)
32 weeks	40.5 cm	(16 in)	1.6 kg	(3.5 lb)
36 weeks	46 cm	(18 in)	2.3 kg	(5 lb)
40 weeks	51 cm	(20 in)	3 kg	(7 lb)

The human embryo requires approximately 280 days to reach maturity.

Assessment of Fetus in Utero

Midwives working in the less well developed areas of the world must rely on the time-honoured means of assessing the normal development of the fetus by relating the estimated period of gestation with the inspection, palpation and auscultation of the mother's abdomen. These methods are valuable even for those living in a highly industrialised society and must never be decried. Nevertheless, modern technology has given us more scientific methods of assessing the well-being of the fetus, and these can often be used to reduce fetal mortality and morbidity rates.

1. *Measurement of Oestrogenic Hormone Levels.* Levels in maternal blood, urine and amniotic fluid give an indication of placental function and growth of the fetus.

2. *Ultra-sound Machines.* These machines can record the fetal heart as early as the ninth week of pregnancy and can be used to plot the position of the fetus and placenta, as pulsations of blood in vessels are recorded.

3. *Amniocentesis.* This has been previously mentioned as a method of diagnosing sex and normality of the fetus or as a route for intraperitoneal transfusions for the fetus.

4. *Radiography.* Large doses of X-rays are harmful to us all, but particularly to the fetus in utero. Used wisely, though, they can diagnose position and assess maturity of the fetus by measuring size and bone density.

5. *Fetal Blood Sampling.* During labour samples of blood removed from the fetal scalp veins can be assessed for pH levels, thus indicating whether or not fetal distress is present.

Multiple Pregnancy

While this term is commonly taken to mean twin pregnancy, there have recently been instances of as many as eight live babies being delivered at the end of pregnancy. There is no doubt that the incidence of multiple pregnancy has increased since the use of drugs to stimulate ovulation in infertile women.

Twins

A twin pregnancy may result from the fertilisation either of a single ovum or two ova.

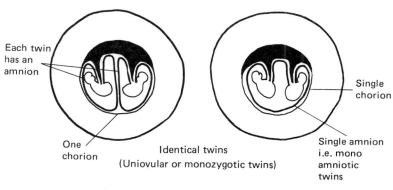

Each twin has an amnion

One chorion

Single chorion

Single amnion i.e. mono amniotic twins

Identical twins
(Uniovular or monozygotic twins)

Figure 11.4
Fraternal and Identical
Twins

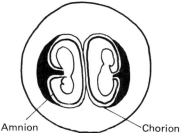

Amnion

Chorion

Fraternal twins
(Binovular or dizygotic twins)

Bin-Ovular Twins

Often referred to as non-identical or di-zygotic twins. The tendency for a woman to produce more than one ovum each month tends to be hereditary, unless drug induced. These twins therefore tend to be familial. Each ovum is fertilised by different sperm and the twins may therefore be of the same, or of different sexes and be no more alike than any other two siblings. In the uterus, they each have their own placenta, amnion and chorionic sac.

Uni-Ovular Twins

Such twins are really an abnormal occurrence. Fertilisation of an ovum takes place in the normal way but the zygote divides into two, resulting in two cells each with a nucleus containing identical chromosome patterns. These twins are often referred to as identical or mono-zygotic twins, being alike in every way. In the uterus they share the same placenta. The actual stage at which the zygote divides seems to vary. Sometimes it is believed to occur after formation of the amniotic sac so that the twins share even the same amnion. Because this is not a normal occurrence one or both twins are more likely to have a congenital abnormality. Siamese, or conjoined twins, would of course be uni-ovular.

THE FETAL CIRCULATION

During intra-uterine life, the lungs of the fetus are inactive and interchange of oxygen and carbon dioxide takes place through the placenta. Extra structures are therefore present in the fetal circulatory system which become useless once the extra-uterine function of respiration is established.

Before the fetal circulation can be fully understood, the general structures and principles of the adult circulation must be brought to mind.

The Adult Circulatory System

Venous blood from the lower limbs is returned to the right auricle of the heart by the **inferior vena cava**, and venous blood from the upper extremities is returned to the right auricle by the **superior vena cava**.

From the **right auricle**, blood passes through the tricuspid valve to the right ventricle and is then pumped to the lungs for replenishment of oxygen by the **pulmonary artery**. Four **pulmonary veins** take the newly oxygenated blood from the lungs to the **left auricle** of the heart where it passes through the mitral valve into the left ventricle.

From the left ventricle, the **aorta** sends blood in to two streams; the ascending branch supplies the head and upper limbs, the descending branch supplies all parts of the body below the level of the diaphragm. Following its circulation to upper and lower extremities, the blood is returned again to the heart by the superior and inferior vena cava.

Additional Structures in Fetal Circulation
(Figure 11.5)

1. *Umbilical vein*: carries oxygenated blood from the placenta to the under surface of the liver.
2. *Ductus venosus*: leaves the umbilical vein before it reaches the liver and transmits the greater part of the newly oxygenated blood into the inferior vena cava, so bypassing the liver.
3. *Foramen ovale*: is an opening which allows blood to pass from the right auricle into the left auricle.
4. *Ductus arteriosus*: a bypass extending between the right ventricle and the descending aorta.
5. *Hypogastric arteries*: two vessels which return blood from the fetus to the placenta. In the umbilical cord they are known as umbilical arteries.

Fetal Circulatory System
(Figure 11.5)

The umbilical vein carries blood, rich in oxygen, from the placenta to the under surface of the liver. The **hepatic vein** leaves the liver and returns blood to the inferior vena cava.

The ductus venosus branches from the umbilical vein and transmits the greater amount of oxygenated blood into the inferior vena cava.

Figure 11.5
The Fetal Circulation

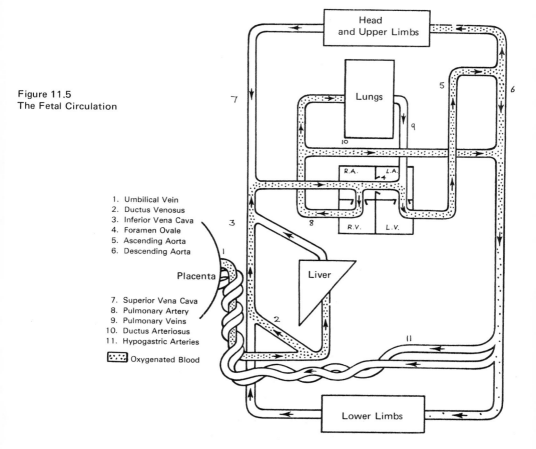

1. Umbilical Vein
2. Ductus Venosus
3. Inferior Vena Cava
4. Foramen Ovale
5. Ascending Aorta
6. Descending Aorta

Placenta

7. Superior Vena Cava
8. Pulmonary Artery
9. Pulmonary Veins
10. Ductus Arteriosus
11. Hypogastric Arteries

Oxygenated Blood

The inferior vena cava, already transmitting blood which has circulated in the fetal lower limbs and trunk, is thus joined by blood from the hepatic vein and ductus venosus and takes it to the right auricle of the heart.

The foramen ovale allows the greater part of the oxygenated blood in the right auricle to pass to the left auricle, where it is then passed through the mitral valve to the left ventricle and then through the aorta into its ascending branch to supply the head and upper extremities. It can be seen, therefore, that the liver, heart, and brain receive the best supply of the newly oxygenated blood.

The superior vena cava returns blood from the head and upper extremities to the right auricle. This with the remainder of the stream brought in by the inferior vena cava passes through the tricuspid valve into the right ventricle.

The pulmonary artery shunts some of this supply of mixed blood to the non-functioning lungs, which fortunately require only a little nourishment.

The ductus arteriosus shunts the greater part of the blood from the right ventricle directly into the descending aorta to supply the abdomen, pelvis, and lower extremities.

The hypogastric arteries which are extensions of the internal iliac arteries carry blood back to the placenta where more oxygen and nutrients are supplied from the maternal circulation.

Changes at Birth

1. The infant cries and expands his lungs, causing an increased flow of blood through the four pulmonary veins into the left auricle. This equalises the pressure between the auricles and the **foramen ovale closes**. With the establishment of respiration **blood is oxygenated in the lungs**.

2. The umbilical cord ceases to conduct oxygenated blood to the fetus and de-oxygenated blood back to the placenta.

3. The **umbilical vein, ductus venosus** and **hypogastric arteries** are now no longer necessary and **fibrose** to form supporting ligaments in the abdomen and pelvis, though the first few centimetres of the hypogastric artery remain patent and become part of the superior vesical artery. By the end of the first week of life, the fetal end of the cord should have dried and separated from the skin of the newly born infant. The **ductus arteriosus** contracts as the lungs expand but does not always close immediately. It gradually **fibroses** to become a supporting ligament in the thorax.

Write an illustrated account of the development of a human embryo using the following headings:
1. The sequence of events following fertilisation and leading to implantation in the uterus.
2. Implantation in the uterus.
3. Increase in length and weight of the fetus from 8—40 weeks.
4. Methods of assessing development of the fetus.

Write a detailed account of the production of:
1. Ovum
2. Sperm.

What is the chromosome number of (1) a gamete (2) a human body cell?

Outline the way in which the chromosome number is reduced and then restored.

Explain the meaning and describe the importance of the following:
1. X and Y chromosomes
2. Meiosis
3. Mitosis
4. Chorionic villi

What additional structures are found in the fetal circulatory system which are not found in an adult? What is their function?

12

The Placenta at Term

Situation

Before delivery the placenta is normally situated in the upper uterine segment. In the third stage of labour it separates from the uterine wall and is expelled.

Shape

It is a flat, roughly circular structure.

Size

Approximately 22 cm (9 in) in diameter. In the centre it is about 2 cm (0.8 in) thick, but becomes thinner towards the circumference. The weight is said to be one sixth of the baby's weight and therefore, on average, varies between 0.5–0.7 kg (1–1.5 lb).

Structure
Maternal Surface
(Figure 12.1a)

In utero, the maternal surface of the placenta lies next to the uterus, deeply embedded in the decidua. On inspection, following delivery, it can be seen that the chorionic villi, which have already been described in some detail, are arranged in lobes or cotyledons, sixteen to twenty in number. The grooves separating the cotyledons are called **sulci**. This surface is dark red in colour, due to maternal blood in the spaces between the villi and to fetal blood in the vessels within each villus. At full term, the placenta feels rather rough to the touch because, having reached its full development by the twenty-eighth week of pregnancy, it then begins slowly to degenerate. Fibrin is deposited over the villi and deposits of calcium can be seen with the naked eye at term. If a large area of placental tissue is affected and becomes fibrosed and white, it is called an infarct. The area becomes inefficient and ceases to function.

Fetal Surface
(Figure 12.1b)

This faces the baby in utero and is distinguished on inspection by its bluish-grey colour and its smooth, shiny surface. The umbilical cord is inserted into this surface, usually in the centre, and blood vessels can be seen radiating from the cord to be lost deep in the substance of the placenta before reaching its circumference. The amniotic membrane covers the fetal surface and can be stripped back from the chorion as far as the insertion of the umbilical cord. The chorion, being derived from the same trophoblastic layer as the placenta, is continuous with the placental edge and cannot be separated from it.

The Amnion

A tough transparent membrane, the amnion is very difficult to tear. It lines the amniotic cavity, covers the placenta and umbilical cord, and is thought to secrete the amniotic fluid.

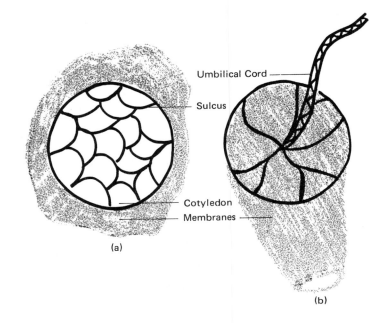

Figure 12.1
The Placenta at Term:
(a) maternal surface
(b) fetal surface

Umbilical Cord
Sulcus
Cotyledon
Membranes

(a)

(b)

The Chorion

This is an opaque, thin, friable membrane, although it does appear to be thicker than the amnion. Because it is so easily torn, small pieces are sometimes detached during delivery and retained in utero.

The Umbilical Cord

At full term is normally 40–50 cm (16–20 in) in length, 1.5 cm (0.5 in) in diameter, and has a twisted appearance; the structure has been described in the previous chapter. It is most often inserted into the centre of the fetal surface, sometimes has a lateral insertion, and is less frequently inserted at the placental edge as a **battledore** insertion. More rarely, the cord is inserted into the membranes with a **velamentous insertion**.

Functions of the Placenta

1. *Respiration.* As the lungs of the fetus do not function before birth, oxygen from the maternal circulation is absorbed through the chorionic villi and passed into the fetal blood vessels. Likewise, carbon dioxide from the fetus is returned to the maternal circulation.

2. *Nutrition.* Break-down products of vital food substances with vitamins and mineral salts are transmitted to the fetus from the maternal circulation. The placenta also stores glycogen.

3. *Excretion.* Waste substances, such as urea and bilirubin, are carried from the fetus to the placenta where they pass through the semi-permeable membrane into the mother's circulation to be excreted by her.

4. *Secretion.* As the chorionic villi embed in the decidua the chorionic gonadotrophic hormone is produced. After the twelfth

week of pregnancy, the developing placenta produces oestrogen and progesterone to maintain the pregnancy and replaces the corpus luteum.

5. *Protection.* The placenta acts as a barrier against most harmful substances, and therefore offers a measure of protection to the developing fetus. However, the virus of rubella and the syphilitic spirochaete can both be transmitted, as also can some drugs such as sedatives and anaesthetics. There is also a leakage in both directions of some blood cells which is why haemolytic disease of the newborn is caused.

6. *Stabilisation.* The chorionic villi, which pass deeply into the decidua, anchor the placenta firmly, stabilising the structure which is so vital for fetal development.

Abnormalities of Placental Development
Placenta Succenturiata
(Figure 12.2a)

This is a placenta in which an accessory cotyledon develops away from the main placental structure. Blood vessels travel across the membranes connecting the succenturiate lobe with the main placenta. Two complications might arise in association with this abnormality:

1. The accessory lobe might be retained in utero when the placenta is expelled, giving rise to post-partum haemorrhage and/or uterine infection and secondary post-partum haemorrhage.
2. Fetal anoxia can be caused either by the presenting part of the fetus pushing on to the vessels connecting the lobe with the placenta, or by the membranes rupturing and involving the vessels.

Vasa praevia is the term used to describe blood vessels which lie below the presenting part. If the membranes rupture, involving these presenting blood vessels, there is consequent danger to the fetus because of blood loss.

Placenta Bipartita
(Figure 12.2b)

Two separate areas of placental tissue develop but there are no connecting blood vessels between them. There is one umbilical cord which divides sending a branch to each lobe, thus distinguishing this abnormality from twin placentae where two cords would be present. No complications are likely to arise with this abnormality: it is mentioned purely out of interest.

Placenta Circumvallata
(Figure 12.2c)

During development, the amnion and chorion double back around the circumference of the placenta giving the appearance of a collar. The chorion is, therefore, still continuous with the edge of the placenta but its attachment is folded back on to the fetal surface. As a result, the edge of the placenta is more easily detached from the uterine wall and may cause ante-partum haemorrhage, the actual causation not being recognised until the placenta is examined at the end of labour.

Placenta Velamentosa
(Figure 12.2d)

Also known as velamentous cord insertion, this is an abnormality of cord insertion rather than of placental development. Because

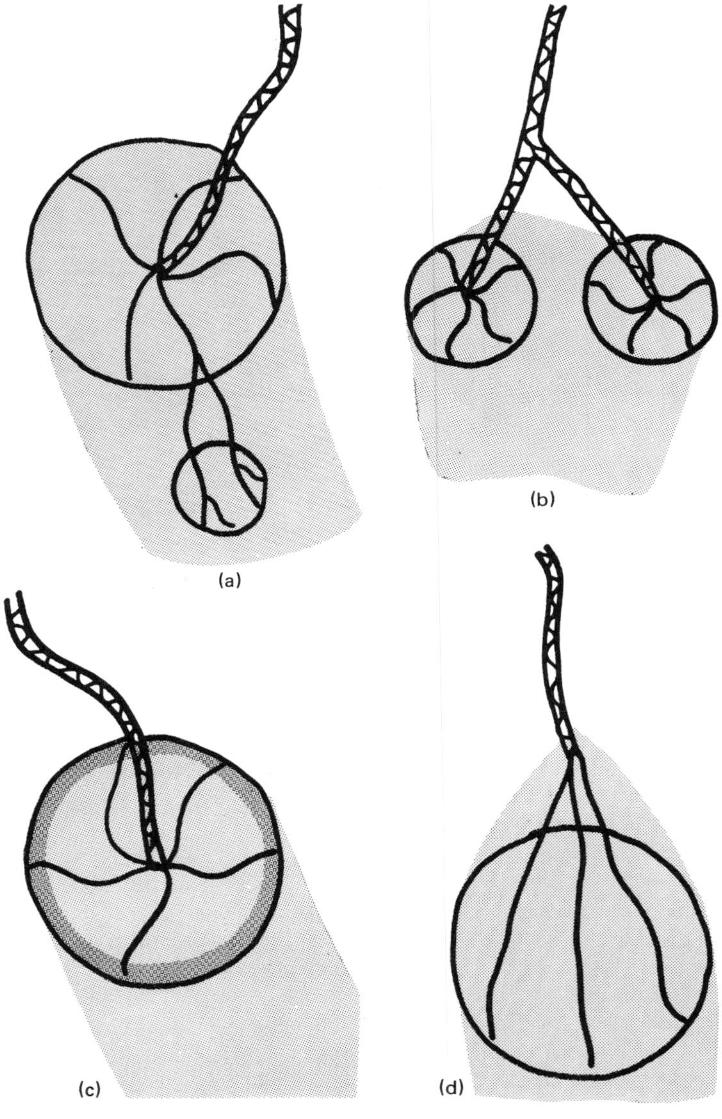

Figure 12.2
Some Abnormalities of
Placental Development:
(a) placenta succenturiata
(b) placenta bipartita
(c) placenta circumvallata
(d) placenta velamentosa

the cord is inserted into the membranes, blood vessels travel from the cord to the placenta across the membranes. The dangers of this condition are those of vasa praevia—pressure on, or rupture of, blood vessels leading to fetal anoxia.

Placenta Praevia
(Figure 12.3)

This is an abnormality of developmental position rather than of placental development, and is therefore mentioned only briefly. It occurs when the placenta is lying either partly or wholly in the lower uterine segment. Four types are usually described.

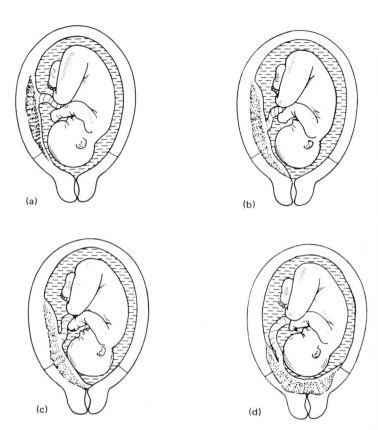

Figure 12.3
Placenta Praevia
(a) Type 1. Placenta lies partly in lower uterine segment.
(b) Type 2. Placenta mostly in lower uterine segment. Reaches to margin of internal os.
(c) Type 3. Placenta lies partly over the internal os.
(d) Type 4. Placenta lies centrally over internal os.

The risk to the fetus is dependent upon the degree of placental separation and consequent blood loss as the uterus contracts. Clearly, with types 3 and 4, elective Caesarean section is always the chosen method of delivery.

Pathological Conditions of the Placenta
Hydatidiform Mole

During the first few weeks of placental development there is a proliferative growth of the chorionic villi and each tiny root-like structure terminates in a sac of fluid. Because of the rapid growth of the trophoblastic layer, the inner cell mass is absorbed and the fetus does not develop. The mole increases in size much more rapidly than the fetus would develop and the size of the uterus is therefore much greater than the period of amenorrhoea suggests. Due to proliferation of the chorionic villi, the amount of chorionic gonadotrophin is greatly increased and a pregnancy diagnosis test will be positive even at 1—100 dilution. Diagnosis is made on the result of this test following the occurrence of vaginal bleeding, also taking into consideration the patient's history which includes a feeling of general ill health and excessive morning sickness. Pre-eclampsia often develops as early as the sixteenth week of pregnancy. In approximately 10 per cent of patients there is a risk of malignancy (chorioepithelioma), and if spontaneous abortion does not occur the patient is admitted to hospital for the uterus to be evacuated.

Urine tests are then carried out over the next two years to estimate the chorionic gonadotrophin levels. During this time the patient is advised not to become pregnant. The chorionic gonadotrophin levels should remain low. Should the levels in urine or blood samples rise then hysterectomy is carried out if the patient is certain that she wants no more children. Alternatively treatment by chemotherapy is indicated and has proved successful. Drugs are continued until two months after the chorionic gonadotrophin levels have returned to normal.

Premature Degeneration

Maternal diseases such as essential hypertension and renal disease cause a narrowing of the lumen of blood vessels and the blood supply to the placenta is therefore diminished. Inadequate placental development occurs, and large areas of tissue may die leading to fetal death and the termination of pregnancy before the twenty-eighth week.

Infarcts

It has already been stated that the placenta begins to degenerate at the twenty-eighth week of pregnancy. More extensive degeneration occurs in association with pre-eclampsia because the disease causes arteriole spasm and large infarcted areas result in placental inefficiency. Labour is usually induced before term because the fetus fails to grow in utero, and further degeneration of the placenta might result in fetal death before or during labour.

When pregnancy is prolonged for more than forty weeks, extensive calcareous degeneration occurs of the post-mature placenta and this too can cause fetal anoxia before or during labour.

Oedema

A large pale water-logged placenta, which may weigh as much as half of the fetus, is always associated with severe haemolytic disease of the newborn. The term used to describe the oedematous fetus is **hydrops fetalis.**

Excessive Size

1. A large placenta is found in association with syphilis when it is also described as being pale and greasy looking. On microscopic examination spirochaetes may be found and the chorionic villi have a characteristic appearance which is readily recognised by a technician.
2. It is sometimes said that the placenta of the diabetic mother is larger than the normal, but this is not always true. When found in association with the large fetus of the diabetic mother it is most probably due to the growth factor of the pituitary gland.

From this brief outline of anatomical and pathological abnormalities of the placenta, it can be seen that following the third stage of labour the placenta and membranes should be very carefully examined to see that all is normal and complete. Labour cannot be said to be completed satisfactorily until this examination has been carried out and observations reported on the patient's notes. Such information is of great importance when considering the management of future labours.

Describe the functions of the placenta. How may the efficiency of the placenta be impaired?

Describe the appearance of the normal placenta at term. What anatomical and pathological changes may be seen in the placenta?

Describe the placenta at term. Enumerate its functions.

Describe the umbilical cord. What should a midwife do if the cord prolapses?

Describe a twin placenta at term. Why are the placenta and membranes so carefully examined after delivery?

Describe the structure of the umbilical cord. What complications involving the cord may be dangerous to the baby?

Describe the placenta. What abnormalities might occur? What is their significance?

What are the functions of the placenta? How may placental function be monitored in pregnancy?

13

The Fetal Skull

Unlike most other bones, the bones comprising the vault of the fetal skull are formed from membrane and not from cartilage. In this membrane are five points called ossification centres (Figure 13.1a). As pregnancy advances, calcium is laid down around these centres and so the skull bones begin to develop. Calcification begins as early as the fifth week following conception (Figure 13.1b).

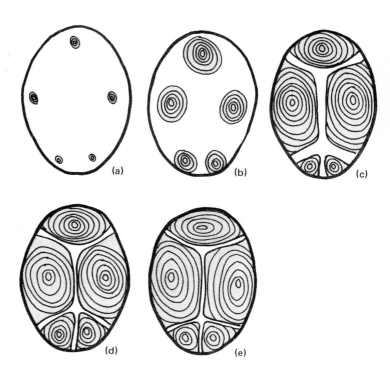

Figure 13.1
Development of Fetal
Skull

When a premature infant is born, the bones are still far from being completely ossified and the head is said to feel rather like a table tennis ball because it can be indented. Intra-cranial damage is much more likely to be sustained during premature delivery because of the soft bones and the wide gaps of membrane still left not ossified (Figure 13.1c).

At full term there are still narrow areas of membrane between the bones where ossification is still incomplete. The bones are harder than those of the premature infant and this head is compared with the hardness of a tennis ball. Incomplete ossification is advantageous because it allows the skull bones to overlap slightly when the head is compressed and pushed through the pelvis by uterine contractions (Figure 13.1d).

Further ossification of the skull occurs if the fetus remains in the uterus for longer than forty weeks. Consequently, not only do the bones become more dense and hard, but the areas of membrane between them are very narrow indeed. When the head is compressed during labour the bones cannot overlap so easily and delivery is therefore more difficult and there is an increased risk of intra-cranial damage (Figure 13.1e).

For descriptive purposes, the fetal skull is divided into three regions:

1. *The vault*: the area above an imaginary line drawn from the nape of the neck to the orbital ridges. A knowledge of its features is very necessary for the practice of obstetrics, because it is the largest part of the fetus to pass through the birth canal and usually comes first (Figure 13.2).
2. *The face*: the area extending from the orbital ridges to the junction of the chin and neck. It is composed of fourteen bones which are firmly united.
3. *The base*: the bones in this area are also firmly united and help to protect the brain.

Bones

The occiput. One bone which lies posteriorly. The ossification centre can be easily defined and is called the occipital protuberance.

The parietals. Laterally are the right and left bones with their ossification centres, the parietal eminences.

The frontals. Anteriorly lie the right and left frontal bones whose ossification centres are not named.

Sutures

A suture is an area of membrane which has not ossified.

(*a*) *Lambdoidal suture*: lies between the occiput and the parietal bones.
(*b*) *Sagittal suture*: divides the parietal bones.
(*c*) *Coronal suture*: separates the parietal from the frontal bones.
(*d*) *Frontal suture*: divides the frontal bones.

Fontanelles

These are areas where two or more sutures meet. Altogether there are six fontanelles but only two need to be mentioned here.

1. *The posterior fontanelle.* This occurs at the junction of the lambdoidal and sagittal sutures. It is very small and triangular in shape. On vaginal examination, it can be recognised by these characteristics because it will just admit a finger tip and three sutures can be distinguished running into it. When felt on such an

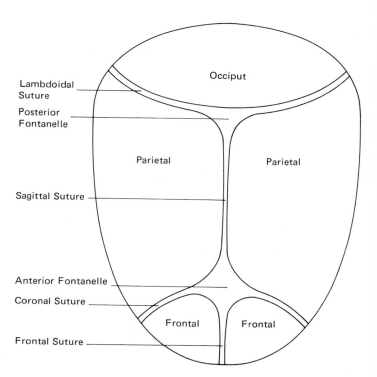

Figure 13.2
The Vault of the Fetal
Skull

examination it indicates that the fetus is lying with his chin well down on his chest and the head is well flexed allowing the smallest circumference of the skull to pass through the birth canal. The posterior fontanelle also indicates the relationship of the fetal skull to one of the four quadrants of the mother's pelvis.

Thus, if the posterior fontanelle is felt on the right side of the mother's pelvis and towards the front, the occiput must be lying in the right anterior quadrant of the pelvis and the fetal position is said to be **right occipito anterior** (*see* Figure 6.2). The posterior fontanelle is normally closed by the time the baby is six weeks old.

2. *The anterior fontanelle.* This is formed where the sagittal, coronal and frontal sutures meet and it is diamond shaped. It is much larger than the posterior fontanelle, being approximately 2.5 cm (1 in) in length and 1.3 cm (0.5 in) wide. The shape and size therefore help to identify it on vaginal examination, as does the palpation of four suture lines, all signs indicating that the head is not well flexed. When this fontanelle is felt on such an examination it proves that the fetal head is not well flexed and a larger circumference is attempting to pass through the birth canal. Labour on this occasion is likely to be prolonged and more difficult. The anterior fontanelle should be completely ossified by the time that the infant is eighteen months of age.

Areas of the Skull

Glabella: the bridge of the nose.

Sinciput: the forehead.

Bregma: the anterior fontanelle.

Vertex: the highest point on the fetal skull.

It lies on the sagittal suture midway between the parietal eminences.

The term vertex is also used to describe an area bounded by the anterior and posterior fontanelles and the parietal eminences.

Lambda: the posterior fontanelle.

Occiput: the area occupied by that bone.

Suboccipital area: lies below the occipital protuberance.

Mentum: the chin.

Circumferences of the Fetal Skull
A Well Flexed Head

When the fetus lies with his head well flexed, the circumference which attempts to pass through the pelvis, i.e. to engage in the pelvis, is the **suboccipito-bregmatic** circumference of 30.5—33 cm (12—13 in). The measurement is taken around the occipital protuberance, the parietal eminences, and the bregma. It is a circular area and passes through the pelvis easily.

An Erect Head

The circumference which engages in the pelvis is the **occipito-frontal** circumference of 33—36 cm (13—14 in). It is measured around the posterior fontanelle, parietal eminences, and the orbital ridge. This is not a circular area but much more ovoid, and labour is more difficult both because of the larger measurement and the shape.

A Partly Extended Head

The circumference which tries to engage in the pelvis is the **mento-vertical**. It measures 38 cm (15 in), and is therefore too large to pass through. It is measured around the chin and up to the vertex and is associated with a brow presentation.

Diameters of the Fetal Skull
(Figure 13.3)

1. *Bi-parietal.* Taken between the parietal eminences and measures 9.5 cm (3.75 in). It is the widest transverse diameter and the fetal head is said to be engaged when the bi-parietal diameter has passed through the pelvic brim.

2. *Bi-temporal.* Measured between the two extreme points of the coronal suture and is 8 cm (3.2 in).

3. *Suboccipito-bregmatic.* The measurement from below the occiput to the bregma. It measures 9.5 cm (3.75 in), and is associated with a normal presentation and position of the fetus, the head being well flexed.

4. *Suboccipito-frontal.* The head is less well flexed and the measurement of 10 cm (4 in) is taken between the suboccipital region and the centre of the sinciput. This head will flex with good uterine contractions and labour is likely to be normal.

5. *Occipito-frontal.* The head is erect. The diameter attempting to engage in the pelvis would be 11.5 cm (4.5 in) and measured between the occiput and the glabella. As well as the larger

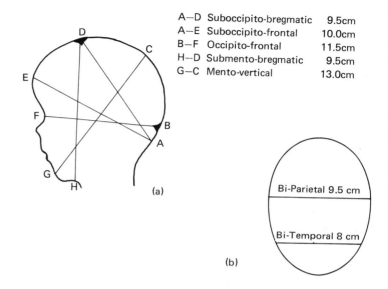

A–D Suboccipito-bregmatic   9.5cm
A–E Suboccipito-frontal   10.0cm
B–F Occipito-frontal   11.5cm
H–D Submento-bregmatic   9.5cm
G–C Mento-vertical   13.0cm

(a)

Bi-Parietal 9.5 cm

Bi-Temporal 8 cm

(b)

Figure 13.3
Diameters of the Fetal
Skull

diameter, the ovoid shape makes it more difficult to get through the pelvis and when the head is in this attitude, labour tends to be prolonged.

6. *Mento-vertical.* The head is partly extended, with the brow presenting. The engaging diameter is measured from the chin to the vertex and, being 13 cm (5.25 in), is the largest diameter of the fetal skull. Vaginal delivery, when the fetal head is in this attitude, is usually impossible.

7. *Submento-bregmatic.* The head is fully extended, and being thrown right back, it is the face which attempts to pass through the pelvis. The measurement of 9.5 cm (3.75 in) is taken from below the chin to the bregma. Although this is a small diameter, labour is usually more difficult because the face bones are firmly united and cannot override; also, the irregular features of the face cannot be applied well to the cervix and cannot therefore stimulate good uterine contractions.

Sutures and fontanelles recognised on vaginal examination will denote whether the head is well flexed, not flexed, or extended. The diameter of the head likely to pass through the pelvis can be calculated and, at delivery, the smallest possible diameter of the skull allowed to pass through the pelvic outlet, thus minimising the degree of injury to the maternal soft tissues. When larger diameters are likely to be delivered, an episiotomy can be performed early enough to prevent more severe trauma.

It is important to note that, like the diameters of the maternal pelvis, those of the fetal skull cannot be measured in real life. X-ray examination is the only way of estimating them. It is important that this knowledge be practically applied during the management of labour.

**The Cerebral
Membranes and
Venous Sinuses**

The cerebral membranes are composed of dura mater, which is the outer of the three meninges covering the brain and spinal cord. It is a tough, fibrous membrane.

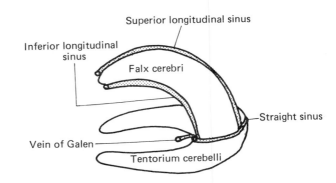

Figure 13.4
Cerebral Membranes and
Blood Vessels

The Falx Cerebri

This is a double fold of dura mater which dips down between the two portions of the cerebrum, the largest part of the brain.

*The Tentorium
Cerebelli*

A fold of dura mater which runs horizontally at right angles to the falx cerebri with which it unites. Being shaped rather like a horseshoe it divides the cerebrum from the cerebellum.

*The Superior
Longitudinal Sinus*

A vessel which runs posteriorly along the convex border of the falx cerebri, increasing in size as it approaches the occipital protuberance. It receives the superior cerebral veins and veins from the pericranium.

*The Inferior
Longitudinal Sinus*

A vessel contained within the free border of the falx cerebri which also increases in size as it runs posteriorly. It receives veins from the falx and there is some drainage into it from the medial aspects of the brain.

The Straight Sinus

This is a continuation of the inferior longitudinal sinus and lies at the junction of the falx and tentorium. It drains not only the inferior longitudinal sinus but also the great vein of Galen.

The Vein of Galen

This joins the straight sinus at its junction with the inferior longitudinal sinus and is made up of many vessels from the brain substance.

During labour, when the fetal head must adapt itself to the shape of the birth canal, these structures are all subject to some degree of pressure as the head changes shape but normally they are able to withstand the stress of a normal vaginal delivery.

Moulding
(Figure 13.5)

This is the term used to describe the change which takes place in the shape of the fetal skull as it passes through the birth canal. Every baby's head is therefore moulded to some extent unless he

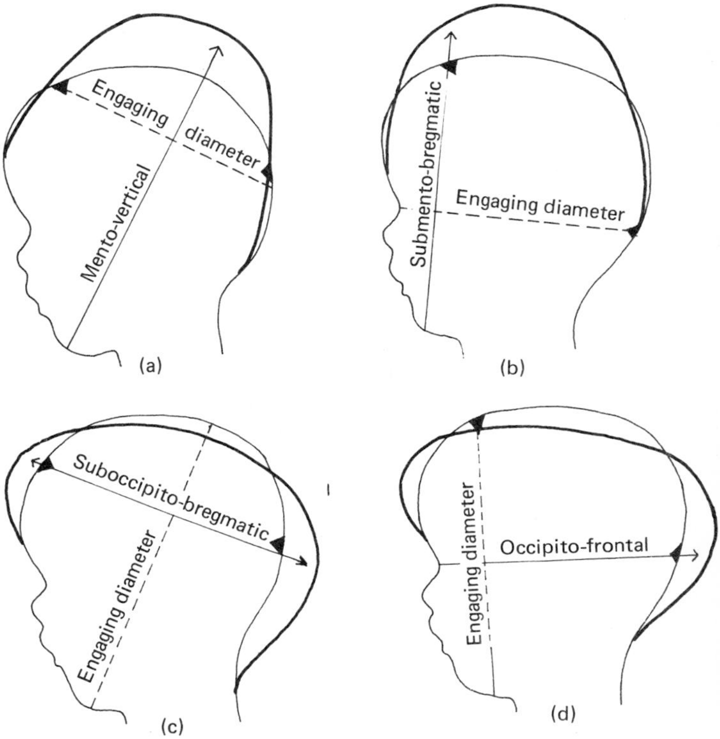

Figure 13.5
Moulding of the Fetal
Skull: (a) well flexed head
(b) erect head (c) partly
extended head (brow
presentation) (d) fully
extended head (face
presentation)

is delivered by elective Caesarean section. As the head descends through the pelvis in response to the downward pressure of uterine contractions so the skull bones overlap each other. The engaging diameter of the head receives the pressure and is therefore reduced in size, while the diameter which lies at right angles to it is pushed outwards to become elongated. The shape of the baby's head following delivery is characteristic of the attitude of the head at the beginning of labour. Providing that moulding takes place gradually without being prolonged, the cerebral membranes and blood vessels are not likely to be damaged.

In certain types of moulding, however, the internal structures are more likely to be damaged. Oedema and congestion may give rise to signs of mild cerebral irritation, while tearing of the membranes with involvement of blood vessels will cause more severe signs and can lead to death or permanent cerebral damage. The dangerous types of moulding are listed:

1. *Excessive Moulding*   This will occur when labour is prolonged, due to disproportion between the size of the fetal head and the maternal pelvis, or where the skull bones are not completely ossified (as in prematurity) and offer little resistance to pressure.

2. *Upward Moulding*

When the occipito-frontal diameter is the engaging diameter, moulding occurs in the submento-bregmatic direction, so that the falx cerebri is pulled upwards. It is then likely to tear at its junction with the tentorium, and rupture of the membranes in this area will also involve the large blood vessels. This type of moulding occurs when the baby delivers face to pubes, and when the after-coming head of the breech passes through the pelvis.

3. *Rapid Moulding*

Rapid compression and decompression of the head is also likely to result in rupture of the cerebral membranes. Rapid moulding occurs in a precipitate delivery, i.e. when labour does not exceed four hours, and during the delivery of the head of a breech presentation, because the head passes through the pelvis in a matter of minutes.

Any infant who has been subject to any of these dangerous types of moulding should be cot-nursed during the first twenty-four hours of life, and carefully observed for signs of cerebral irritation.

The Scalp Tissues

There are five layers of scalp tissue:

1. *Skin*: containing hairs. This is the outer covering.
2. *Subcutaneous tissue.*
3. *Muscle layer*: containing the tendon of Galea.
4. *Connective tissue*: a loose layer.
5. *Periosteum*: which covers the skull bones.

Two conditions involving these tissues can arise during labour and both cause a swelling on the infant's head.

Figure 13.6
(a) caput succedaneum
(b) cephalhaematoma

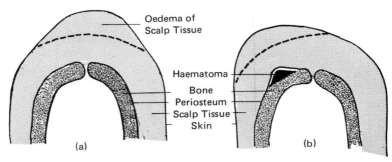

1. *Caput Succedaneum* (Figure 13.6a)

This is an oedematous swelling of the subcutaneous tissues of the fetal skull. It occurs following early rupture of membranes in the first stage of labour because there is no bag of forewaters to take the pressure of the dilating cervix of the fetal head.

−Characteristics

It is present at birth, and occurs on the part of the head which lies over the internal os, therefore it may lie over a suture line.

Because it is an oedematous swelling, it pits on pressure. It disappears completely within twenty-four to forty-eight hours.

No treatment is required unless the caput is of excessive size, and then the infant should be cot-nursed for at least twenty-four hours and carefully observed for signs of cerebral irritation.

2. *Cephalhaematoma*
(Figure 13.6b)

This swelling is due to bleeding between the skull bone and the periosteum which covers it. The bleeding occurs due to friction between the skull bones and the periosteum as over-riding of the bones takes place during moulding. It is just as likely to occur during a normal delivery as when a more difficult labour occurs. A low prothrombin level is probably a contributory cause.

—Characteristics

It is not present at birth but appears two to three days afterwards, when the amount of blood is sufficient to form an obvious swelling. The swelling is limited by the periosteum and can therefore only occur over a bone, although it may be bi-lateral. It cannot lie over a suture. The head is usually more red and bruised in appearance than with the caput succedaneum. The swelling may increase and takes six weeks at least to disappear completely.

Treatment is only required if the haematoma increases in size over a number of days. Vitamin K injections are then given to raise the prothrombin level and assist clotting. The haemoglobin level should be estimated and the baby treated for anaemia if necessary.

SPECIMEN
QUESTIONS

Describe the anatomy of the fetal skull. What is moulding, and why does it occur?

Write brief notes on:
1. The vertex of the fetal skull.
2. Caput succedaneum.
3. Cephalhaematoma.

Describe the vault of the fetal skull. How may a knowledge of its features be of value in assessing the course of labour?

How may a child's head sustain injury during spontaneous delivery? What symptoms would suggest intracranial injury, and what are the midwife's duties in such a case?

Describe the fetal skull. What changes and injuries may occur as a result of labour?

Write short notes on:
1. Engagement of the fetal head.
2. The occipito-frontal diameter of the fetal skull.
3. The added dangers of a breech delivery.

Index